AN INTRODUCTION TO
FIVE DIMENSIONAL
MANAGEMENT

AN INTRODUCTION TO
Five Dimensional
Management

Rod Unger

First Published 1994

Published by Five Dimensional Management
15-17 The Broadway
Old Hatfield
Herts. AL9 5HZ
ENGLAND

ISBN 0 9523903 0 2

British Library Cataloguing in Publication Data. A catalogue
record for this book is available from the British Library.

Editorial design and production by A&S Editors, Oxon.
Cover design by Jeremy Aird.
Typeset in Janson and printed by Hawthorn, Dorset.

This is dedicated to
EILEEN and IAN.

Thank you for the
inspiration and confidence.

ACKNOWLEDGEMENTS

There are so many people I need to thank, not only for their contribution to the basic Five Dimensional Management concept and this book, but also for their support over the years.

Each of these people is well aware of their importance and how grateful I am. Of all of them, I have to mention three: David Jennings and Peter Watson, my business partners and closest friends, and Emmanuel Aharoni for his support from the very first.

FOREWORD

Many books nowadays have a sexist disclaimer, and I want to have one. Yet the problem with everyone so doing is that they begin to sound insincere. When writing this book I have tried to sprinkle 'his' and 'her' around in somewhat equal measure. Certainly there is no intention to be sexist. However, whilst I believe that Five Dimensional Management is of benefit to everyone it is of definite benefit to many women.

We do live in a sexist world. It is getting better but slowly. Women are disadvantaged and have been so for centuries. One of the problems we have today is that they often have a lower self-esteem because of this history. Five Dimensional Management is a vehicle to improve this situation. It will enable the secretary, the housewife, the nurse - often female roles - to be considered in the same way as the predominantly male held roles. It stresses the importance that everyone has in society and uses the same language to describe what we all do in terms of managing each other. Helping each other fulfil ourselves.

CONTENTS

INTRODUCTION

Behind The Theory

As everybody knows we live in a rapidly changing society. For years society developed quite slowly with certain parts virtually untouched. During these relatively stable years various theories and patterns of behaviour proved to be successful; presumably others were tried and forgotten.

During the twentieth century all that changed and we went from being quite stable to being just the opposite. In this new situation, many of the old theories and patterns of behaviours either did not or could not work. Some of these old theories were found to be not quite as good as had been thought. Others could not cope with the changes taking place. A third category also emerged, comprising theories that had to be invented to cope with the new society. The problem with these and with the others was, and is, that the society (i.e. the problem), was still rapidly changing. Hence a new type of theory is now required. One in which the changing society is a part of the theory, thus enabling it to keep pace. Five Dimensional Management is not a panacea to life but it does show what can be achieved and is an example of the kind of flexible theory now required.

Five Dimensional Management only deals with man-management and this book deals mainly with man-management in a working environment. However, the concept can be used in other fields. The specific changes in society that it deals with are several.

First, it embraces modern thinking in psychology. It embraces everything within such subjects as transactional analysis and does not conflict with any in any respect. It does conflict with certain management gurus but mainly because when they talk of management they mean management of all resources. As stated, Five Dimensional Management relates solely to man-management. Another conflict is that certain gurus believe that the formula that created success in the past will automatically work in the future. I often doubt this and I also doubt that they fully understand what caused the historical success. Other gurus seem to be saying that change is stimulating and that a stimulated organisation succeeds. So be it. Virtually all gurus write and talk in a language which I do not fully understand, often using words they invent. I do not believe this is necessary and certainly it is not helpful. Man-management and Five Dimensional Management can be explained in every day, easily understood language.

Five Dimensional Management also embraces empowerment. In fact, it is all about the empowerment of people. Empowering has already become abused by some, allowing them to hide their entrenched ideas behind a new 'buzz' word. To some the empowerment of people is something which bosses do to and for their subordinates.

This is not how empowering is viewed within Five Dimensional Management. The boss has a role to play, ideally, but it is fundamental that the individual concerned already possesses this quality. S/he can empower him/herself. They just have to take that first step, to begin behaving in a different way. How to do so is explained throughout this book.

Another thing 5DM embraces, is combating the media. It is no good the media saying it only reports what happens (if only that was true!) and is not responsible for much of the cancer in our society. Many people can still remember cigarette manufacturers protesting their innocence. The media alone is not responsible for all our ills but it is, in my opinion, a major player.

Years ago when an atrocity was perpetrated most of us knew nothing of it. Developing minds were protected from such news. Those who were exposed were often harmed for life. Nowadays we are all bombarded with atrocities, they come into our house every night.

My 8 year old son knows all about 'scud' missiles, bombs etc and we don't let him see the news on television. The problem is not that the news allegedly only reports what happens; it is all about keeping it in proportion. The media doesn't do this; it gets things out of proportion.It is largely responsible for distorting our view of the world. Much of what we know and learn nowadays comes from newspapers and television into our homes from all over the world. That was not the case 50 years ago. Society has changed. The media is motivated by money, driven by materialism and we have all been adversely influenced. Freedom of speech should not be allowed to excuse lies and distortions.

Over that same period, obviously, we have changed. How could we have stayed the same?

Another thing we have learned, again largely from the media, is that it is easy to criticise. Too easy.

Many people have got into the habit of being critical of others. Again they get it out of proportion, forgetting the many excellent qualities of these same criticised people. At the same time we have got out of the habit of saying thank you, of saying sorry. We have been brought up in a society where this is not common-place, where it is often deemed to be a sign of weakness.

As we have changed in these and other ways, management theories have come and gone. The autocrat of 100 years ago is no longer appropriate. The word 'superior' has been replaced by 'boss'. The charitable welfare officer has evolved into the influential Human Resources Director.

The problem that we had with most management theories is that they all consisted of what 'the boss' does to 'me'. Then, in turn, what 'I' do to my subordinates. Five Dimensional

Management does away with this once and for all. Management is no longer what a boss does, it's what everybody does.

The chaos of management has emerged because the theories came from a different society. The rapid changes in society distorted the problems because the answers were wrong. We can slow down the apparent rate of change by embracing the changes as a part of the solution; thus we move at the same speed. This is an essential part of Five Dimensional Management.

The final significant factor behind Five Dimensional Management is our enormous belief in the human race. We truly believe that people are, in general, fabulous and that there is almost nothing we cannot achieve in the medium to long term.

Many people have grown up to believe that this sort of outlook is ridiculous. How sad. We believe that everyone can do better by receiving sincere praise when appropriate. We believe that we need to allow others and to be allowed ourselves, to make mistakes and not be pigeon-holed as failures. We believe that people do not want to do a bad job, even though many people do so.

Of course we are talking in generalisation and there are always people who delight in arguing against generalisations by quoting the specific. How clever, how destructive. Our belief is that the vast majority of people are wonderful and that they are also capable of more, of doing better, of fulfilling their potential.

CHAPTER 1

Introduction To Five Dimensional Management

S ome years ago I interviewed a highly intelligent, quick thinking, socially confident graduate. He was in his early twenties and appeared to enjoy being interviewed. However, not having spent much time in the grinding process of making a living, there was little to talk about in terms of work experience and achievement. I was playing for time, wondering how to get him to 'just be himself'.

On being asked how he saw his future, a glazed expression complemented his fixed smile and he replied, "I want to be a manager".

I gritted my teeth, with a mirrored glazed expression substituting for my normally happy smile. I was about to say, "What is a manager and why do you want to become one?" But before I could, the young man carried on by saying, "The problem is, no one will give me a management role without management experience and I can't get management experience without getting a management role - it's Catch 22".

My glazed expression disappeared.

That simple statement set me off on a new train of thought.

In a split second years of studying and man-management

experience were crystallised into what is now called Five Dimensional Management.

I'm sure if someone had told me, that the moment I walked into my first job I was a manager, my route to wherever I was going would have been much easier. Being young and in those days, even innocent, I thought that management was something you aspired to. I know now that isn't true. It's something you do, from a very early age. Babies do it naturally. Almost from birth, they figure out that by behaving in a certain way, someone, usually called an adult, gives them what they want. If a tiny piece of uncontrolled plumbing can get its mother to do what it wants, without even the use of spoken language, getting 'grown-ups' to appreciate man-management can't be that difficult.

Conventional wisdom has it that a manager is someone who is responsible for the work of others. This is too narrow a definition, as will be explained later, and assumes that unless you have subordinates to manage you are not a manager. In Five Dimensional Management our belief is that a manager is someone who takes responsibility for his/her own actions and interactions with others.

The whole concept of Five Dimensional Management is based on this simple definition. Its uses are infinite and practical.

I have read the books and seen the videos of world-renowned authors and speakers who charge a small fortune to let you listen to them pontificate about what they've learnt from the successes and failures of £multi billion organisations. A few questions always come to mind in these circumstances:

a) How do we know that these theories are correct?

b) Even if the theories are correct, how do we know that they're appropriate now and for the future?

c) The number of people who can benefit from these corporate multi national experiences is minimal and limited to the people at or near the top of such organisations. So what use are they to the other 99% of the world?

Ignoring the massive ego-driven personalities of some of these people, ignoring the mystique that they build up around their theories for their own financial benefit, we set out to simplify the whole garbled concept of man-management and to separate it out from management. Furthermore, it is the message being delivered that is important - not someone's ego.

Man-management is a post Second World War concept. We are still using terms and definitions which are over 40 years old. For example, who do you know who nowadays uses the term 'superior'? Very few, as it has inappropriate connotations. We use the word 'boss' which used to be slang but is now acceptable. Things have changed.

For this reason we need to re-evaluate man-management concepts and even the definition of a manager. Not only because the definitions are out of date but because society has changed. And what is society?

We are society and we are demanding that we take charge of our own destiny, not to slavishly work for the 'mill owner' or the autocratic boss from cradle to grave.

Bigger, fitter, better educated, more experienced. We have evolved. Forty years ago was a lifetime in the past. It's history. But don't get us wrong. We're not saying that everything old is bad and needs to be replaced. But we are saying that to keep pace with society our theories need to be continually questioned, evolving and improving.This philosophy is an essential part of Five Dimensional Management.

Why is it we accept that the moment we buy our new sound system or computer, it's already out of date yet we seem to believe that the management of people does not move at a similar pace. People change, their potential is enormous, the ability of the human race should never be underestimated. We all owe it to each other to get as much out of each other as possible, so that we are all fulfilled, having achieved our very best however modest that may be.

Age and experience are no guarantee of effectiveness. Those

without either may often come up with best ideas. Equally there are times when those with the age and experience come up with best ideas. Don't just rely on experience, don't just rely on youth. Use everything and everybody when appropriate. No one person has all the answers. Keep an open mind.

Management gurus talk about management and IBM, Apple computers, ICI, MacDonalds and other large mega organisations, using such words as 'symbiosis'! Fine, they are not talking about man-management, and worse, they are using words I don't understand. Most people don't and can't relate to what they are talking about. Even if they do, they can't take it to work with them the next day and use what little they have learned.

These people are only interested in selling themselves. With 5DM the messenger is secondary to the message and the message is deliberately simple, pragmatic and yet challenging. By this we mean the implications of this management message are far reaching. 5DM gives everyone a language and the basic, simple tools they can utilise from day one, every day.

But why should we want to be a better manager or even a manager at all? Firstly, we are all managers, whether we like it or not. Secondly, it's fun. It's interesting, it's challenging and you don't need anyone's permission to do it.

And finally, without advocating a materialistic attitude, it's the most common way to earn more money, to improve our quality of life. If you don't want to earn more money and be a better manager, then fine. That's your decision, your right.

Too often our first experience of man-management was our first boss. Very often the experience was not a good one and too often we've said,

"When I become a manager, I won't do it that way".

Too often managers have had no formal management training. Unfortunately, because these bosses are the only role models we've had, we act in the same way.

8

Even today you can ask some people in business what a manager is or does and they won't know. Or they will talk about reporting, control, subordinates and all the usual old fashioned terms. These terms are not necessarily wrong but they are incomplete. What they do, is pigeon-hole the manager to be something far narrower than he should be.

Since these definitions were first put forward, society has changed, people have changed and business has certainly changed. Now that much of the world is more affluent, people are better educated and have higher expectations, it is no longer acceptable to manage by what could be construed as exploitation or by being autocratic.

The time has come to reconsider such definitions in the light of this modern world.

Managers are no longer perceived as people who are automatically given respect. Respect can only be earned. Equally, the concept that a manager is someone responsible for the work of others, is inadequate. It might be convenient for some bosses to think like that but how can it be true?

In striving to reach a satisfactory definition we first need to look at what managers do. Here we can accept some convention. We agree that managers communicate, motivate, plan and measure - but what we have done is look at these from another perspective.

In other words we say that anybody who communicates, motivates, plans and measures is a manager and that includes EVERYBODY. Simple, isn't it?

Five Dimensional Management is a concept whereby everybody learns to appreciate they are managers. They appreciate who they are managing, how to manage them and how to measure their success in the process.

Everybody, but everybody, is a manager - in any situation. Everybody has at least four areas or dimensions of management responsibility, many people have all five. Again, our definition of a manager is 'someone who takes responsibility for his/her own actions and interactions with others' and this means everybody. These five dimensions are identified and examined in depth later in the book.

So as an example, consider: if you communicate with someone you are managing them. Your chosen method of communication, the information you choose to communicate and not to communicate means you are managing. The language, vocabulary and method chosen means you are managing.

In addition to the four conventional man-management skills - communicating, motivating, planning and measuring - we have added one other skill. We believe that all managers, i.e. everybody, sells. Everybody in their working, managerial life has to sell an idea or has to persuade someone to do something; we call that selling. It's not a word that everybody likes but we want you to learn to appreciate it. Later on we will explain how and why.

Linked to this is one word we don't like as we believe it is inappropriate nowadays. It is the word 'delegate'. We believe this refers only to the boss/subordinate management style of yesteryear. We believe it has been replaced by the word 'sell', or as someone else suggested, roll the two words together to create the word 'selegate'. For a good boss to get a subordinate to do something, he has to sell the idea. Again this will be examined in depth later in the book.

So that there is no misunderstanding, we should now define what we mean by these five management skills, although our use of the words will become clear as you read the book.

1. *Communicate*
   Getting the right message to the right person at the right time in the right way to get the right results.

   Everyone knows it's important. Some people still don't do enough, won't change and don't know whether they are good at it or not. Communication is to do with effectively transmitting required information.

2. *Motivate*
   The process by which someone does something because they want to.

   In 5DM we believe that we cannot motivate people. We believe that everyone is self motivated. Some people more than others, but nevertheless everyone is self-motivated to some greater or lesser extent. What we managers can do is create opportunities and environments, we can provide the tools to allow people to achieve and even exceed their expectations.

3. *Plan*
   Determining the most effective way of co-ordinating and actioning those resources needed to complete a task.

   If you don't plan you can't manage. Time is important. A degree of self-discipline is important. To appreciate your own and other people's time, priorities and needs is important.

4. *Sell*
   To motivate someone to buy an idea, product or service that they want.

   Selling is not a popular word in the UK. It is far more popular in other countries, notably the United States. This in itself is enough to put some people off.
   Selling is *not* getting people to buy something they don't want. Nor is it ripping somebody off by using clever words designed by some clever advertising agency.
   Selling *is* honestly persuading people that it is in their interests to do something. Selling is being able to justify

decisions made. If you can't justify why Jenny earns more than Sally then she probably shouldn't. Sally may not like the reasons but at least she should appreciate that there is a logic.

5. *Measure*
To determine how effective you are as a 5DM manager.

If we said everything can be measured someone would come up with something that couldn't be. So to save them the trouble let us say that most things can be measured.

Some people have a problem with agreeing that something has been measured without the use of a ruler or a mathematical solution. Life isn't like that. Some things, including managerial performance, cannot be measured so objectively. But we can become accurate enough to obtain relevant results and make use of them.

Managers - and that means all of us - should always be measuring our own performance. We should also be helping everyone around us to measure themselves. Measuring is not something which bosses do secretively on someone and then store away the results to use when it suits their purpose.

Measuring is to do with you achieving pre-determined agreed objectives and then deciding how you can do better - if you want to. If you don't want to or if you're satisfied, then so be it.

It is fundamental to Five Dimensional Management that no one can make you do better, only you can do that. What Five Dimensional Management can do is make you happier with the decision not to try, if that's what you've decided. Five Dimensional Management will make you make such decisions consciously and come to terms with the implications of those decisions.

Within Five Dimensional Management we assist you in obtaining the views of people who know you and your current man-management capability. We do this by enabling you to make use of questionnaires which you draw up. It is essential to obtain the honest and constructive views of others.

At the same time you should complete the same questionnaire

yourself as to your own strengths and weaknesses. You will then have an average score of your colleagues and can compare it with your view of yourself. If you are a good manager you will be fairly accurate. Either way, you should learn something useful!

Only then will you have genuinely measured your performance and hence only then can you determine your training needs and take the necessary action. Only then will you improve as a manager.

Five Dimensional Management is easy, it's simple, it can and should be practised everywhere, all the time. And we make no apologies for making the statement that it's irrefutably obvious. The best things in life are the simplest.

So, to the young man who walked into my office so many years ago and whose name I have long forgotten, thank you. Without you, this book and Five Dimensional Management would never have happened.

SUMMARY OF CHAPTER ONE

The Five Dimensional Management definition of a manager is:

'Someone who takes responsibility for their own actions and interactions with others'.
EVERYONE IS A MANAGER.

As Five Dimensional Managers we all do the following five things:

1. Communicate

2. Motivate

3. Plan

4. Sell

5. Measure

CHAPTER 2

The 5DM Golden Rule And Conscious Decisions

Now that we have agreed that everyone is a manager and we know what managers do, why are there so many books, videos etc on man-management?

One of the reasons is because we all have unique personalities and, therefore, we all need to be managed differently. You will probably have heard this before but just knowing the problem doesn't help.

If you try to treat everyone the same way, you will fail as a man-manager. It has been argued that the most successful people in business have been autocrats. We would argue that they possibly were not, but that they appeared to be so to lesser people. We would also argue that they had other talents, such as being exceptionally intelligent and highly motivated.

But even if they were, so what? Society has changed. Today's business heroes are not autocrats. They are achieving because consciously or not they have kept up with today's society. Richard Branson of Virgin and Bill Gates of Microsoft spring to mind.

As a generalisation we are mere mortals of average intelligence needing to manage everyone differently. But how? It seems so difficult, it's so much easier to always be an autocrat or an indecisive wimp and to treat everybody the same. If you want to continue in that way, so be it. Do so consciously and in the knowledge that you are not a good manager and that you should not have aspirations of going up the managerial ladder. And not everybody should want to go up the ladder.

The way to manage everyone appropriately is to remember the 5DM Golden Rule which comes from the saying (slightly paraphrased):

"Do unto others as they need to be done by."

Put into a management context this becomes:

"Manage people the way they need to be managed."

By this we mean that if you are, for example, trying to manage an autocratic person, then be strong, direct. Agree with him or her set goals with challenging time limits. If you are managing an expressive, chatty person, give him or her time to have their say. Give them praise, rewards, make them feel involved. Both of these people have strengths and weaknesses, both are valuable, so value them. Try to get the best out of them and don't treat them both the same. We are going to refer to this belief throughout the book.

However, be careful; do not manage people the way they 'want' to be managed. Don't let them tell you how to manage them. Only you have the right to make that decision. You are the manager, you are responsible for your actions. You have to make the conscious decision of how best to manage the individual in question.

All you now have to do, is work out how you can 'read' or determine who it is you are managing. Actually it's not that difficult. By using a few simple rules most people can become much better at it than they presently are, than they imagined. A lot of books have been written about this, some good, some not so good. As a manager with aspirations of going up the management ladder, you should read some of these books and keep up to date with modern thinking.

To know how to manage someone you need to 'measure' their unique personality. Their personality is caused by a complex interaction of experiences etc, but we do not need to know all about this to begin applying the Golden Rule.

Most people who have researched the measurement of personality agree that it consists of four parts. They further agree that most of us have one of these four parts in a greater proportion to the other three. Let's begin by looking at these four main categories, on the following pages, after which we can discuss secondary traits.

CATEGORY A - DRIVER

These people are forthright, they are driving, competitive, ambitious, decisive and often aggressive. They are always direct, no beating about the bush for the 'driver'. They will nearly always go straight to the point. They are often dominating, blunt and overbearing. They have strong self-motivation and nearly always a strong ego.

Tell-tale signs

Very often they sit facing you head-on, especially if they have some respect for you. They ask questions, often in a very direct way. They make demands and they want their demands met now! They are nearly always in a hurry and they set themselves high goals. They often forget to say 'please' and 'thank you'. They nearly always work really hard.

Strengths

Tremendous determination and energy such that they make things happen. They often achieve well in their chosen field. Other people can gain strength from them. They dare to do things and they make decisions quickly.

Weaknesses

They forget that we mere mortals are not as strong and not as ambitious. They don't give enough praise, they can be overbearing, to the extent of bullying. They don't always evaluate risks properly and hence make decisions too quickly. They lack humility. They tell people what to do.

How to manage

You have to be strong, even if you are role playing. You have to stand up to them sometimes, but do so intelligently and choose your moments. Don't expect praise but give them some. If you say you can do something, do it. If you genuinely cannot do what is required, you had better have good reasons and some options.

CATEGORY B - THE DEMOCRAT

Democrats are friendly, affable, chatty and extrovert. They like people and need to be liked. They love praise and are quick to give it; sometimes too quick. They like working in teams and like to make decisions collectively. They are always optimistic, sometimes too much so, especially about themselves and their abilities.

Tell-tale signs

They always try to be happy so when they aren't you really know about it. They wear their heart on their sleeve. They talk a lot and aren't as good at listening. They are always optimistic, for example, about sales figures but do not like having to say exactly where the sales are going to come from. They wear bright clothes. They don't plan well.

Strengths

They are positive, motivational, optimistic and cheerful. They are good communicators and will nearly always bounce back. People like them generally despite their obvious failings. They are persuasive, sympathetic and confident.

Weaknesses

They talk too much and are over-optimistic as to what they can do. They exaggerate. They waste their time and the time of others. They always have good reasons why they haven't achieved. They lack judgement especially in other people.

How to manage

You must give them praise and you must give them time. They need to talk to you, so give them a chance but not too much. Get them to agree what they can do and then use your judgement in reducing their goals for your own purposes. Don't be disappointed when they always do 80% of what they said they would do. Let them bask in the glory of their achievements and don't be too hard on them when they fail; if you do they will seek new pastures.

CATEGORY C - DEPENDABLE

These are the nicest people of all. They are genuine, loyal and sincere. They rarely gain or want the spotlight but they are essential to any team succeeding.

Tell-tale signs

They listen very carefully, they are gentle, patient and lenient. They are not demonstrative or loud but occasionally will surprise you by being quite firm. You will trust them quite quickly.

Strengths

They will very rarely let you down; they don't give or take offence. They are kind, reliable and thorough in what they do. They are patient, accommodating and extremely supportive. They can persist with difficult tasks.

Weaknesses

They lack ambition and only like to do one thing at a time. They often take a little too long and are sometimes too kind, too sympathetic.

How to manage

Don't underestimate them and always remember how valuable they are. They are the 'oil' for the cogs of business. Show your appreciation in a quiet way. Don't embarrass them by giving them too much spotlight. Listen to what they have to say - it won't be a waste of time.

CATEGORY D - DETAILED

These are the diplomatic, precise and very professional people. They are always accurate and very often this means they are cautious. They are logical, which people often misread as automatically being intelligent.

Tell-tale signs

They are always tidy and organised. They have charts, plans, lists which are all detailed and which all logically fit together. They argue in a persistent way by quoting facts. They are diplomatic.

Strengths

They are capable of doing things that need a lot of detail. They get things right. They plan well, they are careful, conservative, adaptable and perfectionists. You can't bully them.

Weaknesses

They go into too much detail when it's not required and they are evasive when straight talking is required. They don't take risks and they worry.

How to manage

Give them the time and the facts. They need to do a job properly. Don't ask them to rush it - they can't. Give them praise by showing appreciation of their work. Explain to them why risks have to be taken.

Hopefully, as you read through these four categories you started recognising yourself and some of the people you know. Some others were probably more difficult. The more difficult ones are probably so because they have two or three of the four traits almost as strong as each other. And it can be any two or three of the four.

Again, as an example, a category A person, the 'Driver', could also be strong in terms of category D. So in addition to being aggressive, achieving and decisive, they could also be very demanding in terms of quality, doing things properly and so on. Another 'Driver', weak in terms of category D, would give very little importance to doing things properly; his or her attitude would be more cavalier and to just "getting it done". More importantly, they would need managing in a very different way.

As you practise this you will get better at it. There are excellent books on the subject explaining the different categories in far more depth than we have here. There are also excellent 'tests' to measure people's personality. In the UK and in some certain industries, such tests are still often not generally accepted. Yet they have been used for well over 50 years and have been independently validated hundreds of times. Used correctly they are very useful. They do not replace your own opinion or gut reaction or anything else. However, if they are abused or taken as being irrefutably correct you will be disappointed.

We should also state that within Five Dimensional Management we are not trying to accurately measure the entire person, nor their personality for that matter. We are trying to give you some help to broadly categorise people to assist you and them in your management of them.

We have not yet made any allowance for intelligence or experience. Obviously you will 'manage' an intelligent person differently to someone not so gifted in this way. Similarly with experienced people. It would be silly to manage the new secretary to the company in the same way you manage Betty, who has been with the company for years. Even if they do have the same personality.

The next 'tool' to have an appreciation of, is one to assist you to make man-management decisions. Whatever you do or do not do means you have to make decisions. Everyone makes some decisions easily, everyone is indecisive sometimes. Equally everyone makes what are considered to be good decisions and what are considered to be poor ones.

Again we use a simple technique to help everyone make better decisions. But before that, let us explain our theory on most business decisions and this includes virtually all man-management decisions. In most cases we do not think it is a case of them being either right or wrong.

If you imagine the 'right' answer, the perfect solution, as being a moving dot in a three dimensional cube, you will have some idea of how we view 'perfect'. It is constantly changing or moving because society is, because what is perfect one day isn't the next. And here we are - another moving or changing dot in the cube, aiming to hit this moving target. Somebody else is arguing with us because they are yet another dot in the cube; they are predicting that the moving, perfect solution will move in a different way to what we are predicting. Big deal. We could both be as right or as wrong as each other.

If we were both aiming in the right general direction, one to the left and one to the right of the perfect solution, then we could both be as 'right' or as 'wrong' as each other.

All this is very well, but we have to make decisions and in fact in Five Dimensional Management we believe we can identify which of these two 'equal' answers will produce the best results.

First, make a decision. Make it as late as is agreeable to allow time to obtain information, for consideration and discussion. But, make a decision within the agreed time limit.

Second, as much as is possible let the person who has to carry out the decision make the decision. Getting back to our example, if the person doing the work wants to go for the solution aiming to the right of our 'perfect' dot and the boss is insisting on the other, he or she will achieve a better result if allowed to 'own' the decision by getting their own way. All other things being just about equal. Again, we will be showing how this works in practice throughout the book. If the boss insists, there will inevitably be some resistance to the idea and the next time the individual is asked for an opinion he or she may not bother.

Before going any further we should say that this in no way conflicts with or overrides making decisions where facts are the central part. Facts (as opposed to opinions, bias, lies etc) should never be ignored. Real facts are irrefutable. But in man-management a deal of subjectivity is inevitable and it is in these cases that our belief can help. Again it is worth repeating that this only deals with man-management and not with other issues or problems.

Very often it is possible to allow someone to make the decision when you 'know' that it is the wrong one. Sometimes with all options having been aired, you can allow someone to make the 'wrong' decision because you know what the damage will be and that it is limited. Afterwards there is no need to say, "I told you so". Intelligent people learn from their own mistakes. Another of the rules behind Five Dimensional Management is:

I hear	and	I forget
I see	and	I remember
I do	and	I understand

If you want to truly learn or you want those you work with to truly learn - 'do', gain experience and true understanding from 'doing'.

All this is a little simplistic and needs to be seen in action which will be done later in the book. But in Five Dimensional Management we believe in this general principle. It does not mean that the bookkeeper should determine the capitalisation of the company nor next year's budget. Within Five Dimensional Management we believe in making decisions as low in the structure as possible. We certainly believe in structures (as again will be explained) but they often have to be flexible ones depending upon a variety of other factors.

Getting back to our technique for making decisions, it is called and is encapsulated within the phrase 'Conscious Decisions'.

Too often people make decisions based upon little creative thought, without having given due regard to all the options. It is too easy to say, "I have managed a similar (or the same) situation before". Or to say, "My boss is just too busy, there's nothing I can do".

We believe that people often make these decisions subconsciously, without appreciating what they are doing. They become lazy and lazy people do not fulfil themselves.

We want people to take conscious decisions. And the simple technique we use is to write down 20 options to answer or assist with the problem! Not two or three or 10, but 20. It's hard to do and you will probably need to obtain the help of a colleague or two. But getting to 20 or more is essential. Being creative and thinking hard is essential and it is good for you!

As an example, when we were explaining Five Dimensional Management to a director of a major corporation, he said that he had a particular problem with a trusted colleague who had recently been promoted and was not meeting agreed timescales on certain key tasks. This director was extremely competent, but he did not know what to do. He said he had given the person in question the authority and resources required and they had agreed on the timescale.

We explained about 'conscious decisions' and in 10 minutes together we wrote down 20 things that the director could do. We suggested 10, the director suggested 10. Within those few minutes the director realised there were two things he could do to manage the problem. All we contributed was the impetus to make him consider other options, make a conscious decision and to have faith in his colleague.

Incidently, our first idea was to ask the colleague why he was missing the deadlines. It's all a lot better than dishing out the expected 'dressing down' or considering demotion.

The third tool you need is to make use of a very simple phrase. It has to be done honestly and sincerely but as often as possible. Most people rarely use it, some don't know how to.

The phrase is "Praise behaviour you want repeated".

As with everything within Five Dimensional Management, it is blindingly obvious and blindingly simple.

When anyone does something well, irrespective of who they are, tell them! Say well done. Whatever it is that has been done, it does not have to be perfect. It only has to be well done by the standards of that person. If an athlete goes to the Olympic Games and produces a personal best performance but does not win a medal that person should receive considerable praise. To run their best ever time is praise worthy but to do so at the Olympics is exceptionally so. Similarly, the day your daughter swims 50 metres for the first time she deserves just as much praise.

If praise is used insincerely or for unworthy matters it will obviously become ridiculous. But too often good work gets no recognition and sometimes even veiled criticism.

Research has shown that many people do not know how to say "well done", "congratulations" or "that was good work". Don't worry too much about getting the words right, just say thank you or whatever springs to mind.

The final tool you need is judgement. Five Dimensional Management is based upon the belief that most people - when they use their brain consciously - have good judgement. Most people think that most of their colleagues have good judgement most of the time. Many people do not trust their own judgement. There are very few rules in life that you can use all of the time in every situation. Judgement comes with making mistakes, gaining experience and making conscious decisions. Be as intelligent as you can and trust your own judgement.

SUMMARY OF CHAPTER TWO

1. The Golden Rule is "Manage people the way they need to be managed".

2. To do this we need to read people to determine whom we are managing - whether they are a Driver, a Democrat, a Dependable or a Detailed.

3. Most man-management decisions are not right or wrong. Ownership is often the crucial factor.

4. To make 'Conscious Decisions' we have to consider 20 options.

5. Praise behaviour you want repeated.

6. Use and trust your judgement.

CHAPTER 3

The Five Dimensions

Having now agreed that we are all managers and having an awareness of the few, simple techniques required, we now need to identify who it is we are managing.

When interviewing the 'bright, young, socially skilled graduate' referred to earlier, if he had realised that he was a manager, who he managed still had to be identified. And again, no apology is made for the simplicity of the answer.

If we accept that we are all managers because we all communicate, motivate, plan, sell and measure, then anyone that we communicate with, motivate etc is being managed and this means everyone. Everyone you communicate with is being managed by you and should be managed in a conscious way. You should appreciate who you are managing and you should be constantly improving your management skills.

All the people you manage in a working environment fall into five categories, i.e. into five dimensions.

As a Five Dimensional Manager, you automatically manage in four dimensions whether it be your first day at work or your last. Many people manage in all five dimensions.

THE FIRST DIMENSION -
THE BOSS

Just about everyone has a boss and everyone should consciously manage their boss. To many people this is surprising and could be threatening. It should be neither.

Virtually every boss I have met is a human being. It's amazing. They have all had strengths, weaknesses, good days, bad days, characteristics, moods etc. And they have all needed managing. Whether they are managed well or not largely depends upon us and how to do it well will be explained later. But why is it so surprising to so many people that they have to manage their boss?

The reason, we believe, is historical and has been perpetuated through the ages almost accidentally. Many people are threatened by their bosses and think of them as ogres. Very few bosses see themselves in that light. Even though some should.

In history, the first 'working' bosses were the land owners, the military generals or other people who literally held the lives of their employees in their hands. Very often these bosses were better educated and could persuade 'the serfs' that terrible things would happen to them unless they did as they were told. Very often if you did not work for that one terrible boss, you didn't work at all and therefore didn't eat.

Over the years society evolved, the work we did changed. We became an affluent society. However, bosses had got into the habit of bossing us around and 'we' had got into the habit of waiting to be told what to do. The boss had got into the habit of not tolerating people who would not do as they were told. Even though legislation and the job market changed, 'we' continued to live in fear of getting the sack, of not being able to eat.

Eventually things changed and will continue to do so. Many people beginning their working career nowadays cannot comprehend that they will ever not be able to eat, nor watch a colour television for that matter. They behave in a different way

29

to their forefathers and therefore have to be managed in a different way.

Nowadays, all intelligent bosses know that they don't hold sway over someone's life and nor do they want to. Nowadays, intelligent bosses do not want to sack anyone, not unless it is really necessary. Sacking someone or making them redundant as it is called is very expensive, particularly if you have to recruit and/or train someone else. The effect upon morale often takes time to get over. It can cause disruption, extra work for people. The company and the boss can get a bad reputation. The customer may not be happy about it etc.

This does not mean that the subordinate can get away with a less than satisfactory performance, because the boss generally does have more power. The boss can affect what we earn, whether or not we get promoted and he may be able to transfer us to a less attractive job. The potential for conflict is real, but it's not in anyone's interest. It's much better that we all manage each other better; that we all get on and do our best, help each other.

In the worse case scenario if your boss really is a pig, then that's what you have to manage. One of the options (and top of most people's list), is to leave, second on the list is to make his or her life a misery. Big deal, who has gained what? If you want to become a manager, if you want to progress in your career, you have to learn to manage problems and people. The less you change your job the better your chance of really getting on.

THE SECOND DIMENSION - INTERNAL COLLEAGUES AND PEERS

Often when we point out to people that they are managing their colleagues, their friends, they object. They don't want to use the word 'manage'. Call it what you may, we call it managing. We want to call it managing because we want to continue breaking down the us and them syndrome. We want to use the same word for your relationship with your non-threatening colleagues as we do for the possibly threatening boss and for all the other dimensions.

Although we are only dealing with the working environment in this book, whenever you communicate with anyone you are managing them. Whenever you try to persuade anyone to do something or to sell somebody something, you are managing them.

Another of the benefits in using this one term is that when you start 'managing' your colleagues you should start improving your management performance. This is achieved by consciously managing them. Not that any of us can do it all the time, of course we all have lapses. But we should try.

This raises another issue; managing people and making conscious decisions is not hard work, it's not onerous. It is, in fact, very creative and involves talking to and involving people we like. It means that we constructively table problems and deal with them, rather than bottling them up. Five Dimensional Management means getting the best of your ideas and the best of others and together making the best of what may be a tough and important problem.

Managing your colleagues is at the very least an opportunity to begin consciously using your new found management skills. It may also improve your working environment, your performance and that of your colleagues and organisation.

But how can you motivate your colleagues, how can you plan and sell to them? As with many others, they may think that all this is the job of the boss. They may resent it if you take over the role of the boss. They may feel you are getting above yourself.

The techniques mentioned earlier provide the way forward and will be discussed in detail in Chapter 6. But in general terms don't do it *to* them, do it *with* them. Give them the problem and let them have the pleasure of helping you. Ask for their help, give them an opportunity to show how helpful they can be and then say "thank you". Done correctly, this cannot be misunderstood as you pretending to be the boss. You don't need anyone's permission as to how you communicate, you don't need anyone's permission to make someone feel good about themselves or to give them praise. And you don't need anyone's permission to ask for someone's help. It's called Five Dimensional Management.

THE THIRD DIMENSION -
EXTERNAL COLLEAGUES

'External colleagues' is possibly a new phrase to you.

Nowadays, for a variety of reasons, more and more businesses use resources, including people that they do not directly own or employ. If you are a computer hardware company, it is highly unlikely that you will manufacture your kit in the UK. If you are a small or medium sized company, it is unlikely that you will employ your own computer expert to resolve your computer problems as they inevitably happen. The reasons for these two examples is that British labour is often too expensive for manufacturing and the expertise of the computer engineer is not required often enough to warrant full time employment.

There are other reasons for making use of external resources, including lack of availability, redundancy, legislation etc.

Years ago this situation was not so common. When it did occur the external resources were often treated as outsiders. This was particularly true in the UK, where providing a service is to this day often looked down upon.

As the use of external people grew, so did their importance. More and more the 'employing' company became dependent upon these external people but it did not have direct control over them; therefore the old-fashioned management techniques were even more inappropriate. Traditional methods were used but proved unsuccessful. These included confrontation, slow payment and dictatorial methods.

During the recession in the UK starting in the late 1980s, another group of external people suddenly became important. In some industries they realised that clients, or customers as many became known, were suddenly worthy of attention. It became important to go and get orders rather than just receive them. Many companies started talking about being user-friendly or client-orientated for the first time. Presumably many such dinosaurs are only waiting for the economy to pick up before they revert to their old, tried and trusted, ignorant ways.

Even when they did try to 'manage' their customers, many only paid lip service to the idea and again used their instinctive, old methods in the absence of any others.

But the working environment has changed dramatically, as described, and therefore we have to keep in step. New management techniques have to be used.

Those external human resources are and always will be vital to the wellbeing of any organisation. Thus they have to receive just as much attention as any other human resource.

As usual we have stated the case in generalisation. In certain industries, for years they have had an excellent relationship with their customers. Equally they have weathered the recession better than many. The manufacture of semi-conductors and pharmaceutical research spring to mind. In general terms, such industries are more sophisticated in terms of management than others and they attract, in general, a better calibre of people. Those two facts are inexorably inter-linked.

THE FOURTH DIMENSION - SUBORDINATES

To traditional managers, man-management is exclusively about managing subordinates or, worse, telling them what to do.

This is the one dimension which everyone knows of. Some people therefore assume that there can be nothing new to learn. Surely all those thousands of books already written have stated whatever can be stated?

Within Five Dimensional Management, we look at things differently and so we manage subordinates in a different way. We treat them as we do everyone else. We do not wish to be perceived as a threat to them, we want to work with them.

As a boss we probably do have more power, more information and possibly more experience. We do have to ensure goals are set, understood and met and we have to fulfil other 'boss' type functions, but we also believe that all our subordinates:

- Are intelligent
- Want to do a good job
- Want to do better
- Often understand the problem better than us
- Would rather not change jobs
- Want to be appreciated
- Have different experiences
- Want to be promoted and/or earn more
- Like helping people - especially those they like
- Would want to be involved in most decisions involving themselves rather than be just told what to do
- Would rather not be told off
- Do not want to be humiliated
- Need help

Regretfully, to many bosses a lot of this will be too idealistic. Worse than that, many others believe they treat 'their' staff in this way and yet nothing could be further from the truth. They have never bothered to get an honest measure of their performance and attitudes. A boss owes it to subordinates, the organisation and to himself to believe in them, all their qualities and to make full use of these talents.

THE FIFTH DIMENSION - YOU

You are the most important person in your life because you are life itself. Whilst you may say your children are or your mother is, without you they don't exist. This belief should not be mistaken for arrogance nor for greed, both of which contradict everything that Five Dimensional Management stands for. But you are a crucially important human resource and you need conscious management.

Everything worthwhile you achieve in life is down to you, everything you don't achieve in life is down to you. If you don't get on in your career, it is your responsibility; if your boss behaves like a pig it is a management challenge for you.

Because we live in a finger-pointing, critical society, it is all too easy to blame someone else. Especially the boss. Don't bother, it achieves nothing. It's all down to you.

If we are not developed or trained, if we are bad at communicating or answering the switchboard, it is our problem and it is within us to do something about it. If we are always negative and complaining we can do something about it. If we are always tired we can do something about it.

Although we are ultimately responsible for what we achieve, we are not alone and so we should not isolate ourselves. It is a fundamental part of Five Dimensional Management that we ask for help and advice from others, that we share our problems, that we help others.

Many of these things have been said before, but life is not a dress rehearsal; this is it. If we don't do it this time around we are going to have regrets later. We have all met people in their 60s and 70s who said they wish they had spent more time with their children, been a better father, climbed Mount Everest etc. Too late. They probably made decisions at the time but without all the facts, without asking for help, without listening. They probably thought they knew best, only to realise they could have easily made better quality decisions by talking to their mother, brother or friend. Not that they should have necessarily always done what their mother said, but if they had explained their problem well and evaluated other options, at the very least they would have been happy with their decisions rather than wondering 'what if?'.

How we should manage ourselves is again explained very simply later on. But in one sentence: be positive, be confident, be aware of your many talents and your humbling inadequacies.

SUMMARY OF CHAPTER THREE

1. We all manage all the time in four dimensions, many of us manage in all five dimensions.

2. The five dimensions are:
   a) The boss
   b) The internal colleague
   c) The external colleague
   d) The subordinate
   e) You

3. By becoming a proficient manager in the four dimensions, one of the many benefits is that we know we will succeed when we manage subordinates.

4. You don't need anyone's permission to be a Five Dimensional Manager.

5. All of us can and want to do better, all we need is a little help.

6. You are responsible for what you achieve.

CHAPTER 4

The 1st Dimension - Managing The Boss

We have explained the theory and techniques behind Five Dimensional Management. We are now in a position to demonstrate how to use them in the everyday working environment.

Earlier we stated that everybody is a manager because they communicate, motivate, plan, sell, measure. We also stated that everybody has at least four dimensions or types of people to manage, with many people having all five.

The first of these is your boss. We believe that most people should have a boss; in fact many need a boss. We do not disagree with some companies who operate a 'matrix' management structure. But we still believe that everyone should have a boss.

Before we can manage the individual in question we need to appreciate why we need one. What use are they?

Bosses invariably have more information than us. However open the culture of a company is, it is not practical for everyone to know everything and all at the same time. So there is the first use of a boss, to obtain information and to pass it on.

The boss has a direct link to his/her boss who has even more information. Because they have more information than you, they can make some decisions that you can't make. Because of that they have power. You too have power so bosses don't have it all. But they often have more power.

Bosses should assist you in carrying out your job. This does not mean solving your problems. They should ensure that you are personally developed not only to cope with your current job but to cope with forthcoming changes in your present job and to cope with your next promotion.

Bosses are not necessarily better people: they do not have to be better paid, although they often are. And nowhere have we stated that they are more important. They just have a different function.

Again, we have to discuss bosses in general but often they have certain similarities. Often bosses, especially good ones, are fairly busy. Generally they have several people and not just you reporting to them. Often, and again especially the good ones, they don't like it when you go to them with problems. They also have likes, dislikes, moods and pressures. They are (generally) human beings.

Going back to reading people, the more we know about our boss and his/her job the better we will be able to manage him/her and the more likely we are to get promoted into that job when he moves. How is he measured? What are her objectives, what sort of pressure is she under?

Write down what your boss does not like you to do in terms of you both doing your job. In relation to those you can affect, don't do them unless you really have to. Equally, write down those things your boss does like you to do and where possible do them as often as possible.

Why is it your boss gets irritable when you go to him/her with a problem? Isn't that what bosses are for? Maybe he/she just wants you to take the initiative? Why not ask?

The way to manage your boss is to go back to the basic rules and techniques as explained earlier in the book.

What category type is your boss? Try to work it out. Ask your colleagues. Ask your boss! Then work out what type of behaviour suits him/her and their management style. Then as much as possible behave like that. Not in an ingratiating way but in a serious, positive and constructive way.

The next stage is to revert to the five skills and consider each one in turn whilst remembering what type of person he/she is and all the other things you know about him/her.

1. *Communication - with the boss*
   Getting the right message to the right person at the right time in the right way to get the right results.

   What is the way that my boss likes me to communicate with him/her? Why is that? What other ways are there? Am I getting the quality of communication that I want? If not, what can I do about it?

   Is he too busy? Why, what can I do to help? How do I know if I'm helping or hindering? What can I do to ensure that I'm helping without taking up more valuable time?

   These could be examples of boss management problems that you have within communication. Another could be he just won't communicate with you. Worse still, could it be she just doesn't like you or has been over promoted and going nowhere? If so, what are you going to do to manage the situation? The answer is to write down 20 options and then make a conscious decision.

   One option could be: "I'm not prepared to do anything about it and because of that I am prepared to put up with the consequences".

   Another could be: "I am going to resign or ask for a transfer".

   But to be a Five Dimensional Manager you have to give consideration to 18 other options and not just your first two. Only then should you make a conscious decision. We would always recommend particularly when taking major conscious decisions to involve a colleague, mentor or friend. You'll often need help to get to 20, not that you have to necessarily take up company time to do so.

Whilst undertaking some Five Dimensional Management consultancy, a customer told us that his boss was just too busy. There was no way he could get his boss to have a meeting. Even when one was arranged it was always cancelled at the last minute and always the reason was entirely valid. Something more important had always happened.

Needless to say, our customer was very frustrated. He felt he had two options; either put up with it or get on with his career elsewhere - resign.

We explained about Five Dimensional Management and asked as to what type of person the boss was. Apparently his primary trait was Democrat.

We then explained about conscious decisions and 20 options and with a little encouragement (and by us asking the right questions) our customer came up with the following 20 options.

1. Do nothing, just put up with it.

2. Get another job and resign.

3. Take the initiative on certain key issues, make some decisions, inform the boss by memo; say that if he had not heard to the contrary within seven days he would be getting on with it. Each decision was to be validated with the options stated and debated.

4. To ask if he could travel with his boss for two days to gain experience of what he did and to use the travelling time to discuss the issues.

5. To invite the boss home for dinner.

6. To invite the boss to his favourite restaurant.

7. To buy the boss a time-management course for his birthday.

8. To ask (by memo) to go on a time-management course, as he realised he was not getting things done as fast as he should.

9. To rewrite his own roles and responsibilities so that he had more decision-making authority, on the basis that the boss was too busy.

10. To talk to his boss' boss confidentially as a mentor and ask his opinion as to what to do.

11. To ask his colleagues as to what to do on the basis that they had the same problem.

12. To start an internal cricket competition on the basis that the boss loved cricket and would move heaven and earth to get there.

13. To buy tickets for the next test match.

14. To ask for a three month appraisal as opposed to an annual one.

15. Ring the boss at his home and just ask him what to do.

16. Just get on and do things and take the consequences.

17. Find out some issues that were taking some of the boss' time and suggest that he could help (as he had plenty of spare time).

18. Get his attention by ringing him up and having a big row.

19. Make a cassette of all the issues so that the boss could listen to them driving.

20. Ask the boss' wife and/or secretary what to do on the basis they know him best of all.

A couple of weeks later we were contacted by our customer who said he had decided to go for numbers 11, 15 and 4, in that order and that the boss had agreed they could travel together for two days. Apparently, the boss had not really appreciated he was holding things up. These two days proved to be very useful and they now have a better working relationship. Having involved his colleagues, our hero was not seen as being favoured; in fact, they had also benefited.

2. *Motivation - of the boss*
The process by which someone does something because they want to.

How can you motivate your boss to achieve his/her objectives? How can you improve the working environment to do so?

First of all you have to know what your boss' objectives are and how he or she is measured.

As an extreme example, let us imagine both you and your boss work in a company where you don't have objectives and your boss' boss is a dinosaur! Come up with 20 options to deal with that one!

Very few bosses we have heard of ever dislike initiative if done carefully. Almost all bosses hate arrogance and you should never go over his/her head unless something legal is involved. So how can you show initiative? Come up with some ideas and determine how receptive he/she is. Don't assume that because you show initiative he/she will let you choose which option to go for. Equally, don't assume that the boss automatically knows better than you.

Between you, you'll reach a good decision. One that you can both own and feel committed to.

If your boss is also a Driver he possibly won't need too much motivation. But he will probably appreciate public acknowledgement. Any public acknowledgement of his achievement would normally be motivational. Such people are also often status driven, so any gift exclusive or expensive would also be motivational. Also, remember, praise behaviour you want repeated.

If your boss is a Democrat, he is more likely to just want praise. Mind you, all bosses should receive praise. Too often subordinates do not feel they can or should do so. Your boss probably wants and needs appropriate praise as much as anyone else, as much as you.

What sort of praise and how it is communicated or delivered are decisions you have to make; more options. But hopefully you have begun to see the enjoyment, creativity and benefit of Five Dimensional Management.

3. *Planning - the boss*
Determining the most effective way of co-ordinating and actioning those resources needed to complete a task.

As with all the skills this one needs to be done carefully and intelligently. As with others it may be a good idea to discuss the problem, if there is one, with a trusted colleague. If there isn't a problem, obviously leave it alone. Don't forget who's the boss.

However, if your boss does need improvement at planning, for example with his/her own time management, then you may have a complex problem. Sometimes it may be difficult to know the real problem so look for the tell-tale signs. Ask the trusted colleague, a secretary, look at his/her desk or work station. If your boss does need improvement in this area, it will almost certainly adversely affect your performance and that of your section/department.

The complexity of the problem is how to improve the situation without giving offence. If your boss is a Five Dimensional Manager, he can be handled in a different, easier way. But let's imagine he is not.

All we have to do is to go back to 20 conscious decisions. Write down 20 things you could do to improve his/her time management. As usual all 20 should be constructive.

As in the earlier example, one option is to buy the boss a two day time-management course.

Another is to ensure that you don't waste his or her time by bothering them with unnecessary matters, or by taking things to them one at a time rather than 10 at a time.

Another initiative that you can take is by determining whether or not a colleague is stopping the boss from taking action and then offer to help the colleague.

By now you should know that you never go to the boss with a problem without having considered all the options and having determined which one you prefer and why.

All these actions need judgement. They all need to be thought through. All options need to be considered, possibly talked through with a confidant before deciding the best course of action. If you make the wrong decision you will soon hear back. Equally, don't expect to please all the people all the time. Sadly, however you try, some people will criticise you for it. When you hear criticism listen to it, evaluate it and the person from whence it came and then decide upon its validity. As a quick rule of thumb, if you have respect for the critic take the advice on board; if you don't respect them, back your own judgement.

4. *Sell - to the boss*
   To motivate someone to buy.

Again this has to be done carefully, with intelligence and only after having made more conscious decisions. Some bosses wouldn't like it if they knew they were being 'sold' to. Others wouldn't mind. Again you have to 'read' your boss - know who it is you are 'selling' to or, put another way, trying to persuade.

One way of selling an idea to your boss that most don't mind, is by going to them with a genuine problem, outlining two or three options as solutions, saying which one you prefer and explaining why. A variation may be to let the boss choose from your three options so that he owns the decision.

Before doing this, you should have gone through all 20 options and as much as possible thought through all objections. It is unlikely that the problem is a totally new one, so precedents must be considered. If you are proposing a new solution then your reasons have to be even better than otherwise.

The benefits in doing this exercise are several. You have not gone to your boss with a problem like lots of people do, you've gone with answers to a problem. Most bosses prefer that. You have shown him or her that you are not only aware of the problem, but that you have considered various alternatives, as opposed to just reacting. You have shown judgement in what to bring to his/her attention. You've shown initiative.

For all these reasons you are likely to gain a favourable hearing, particularly if you have communicated well. Also, because you have given this particular problem quite some thought, you probably know the subject matter better than your boss. The more important the problem, the higher the risk and the more you will have to justify the preferred solution.

Even if your preferred way is not chosen, you are clearly demonstrating your management skills and potential.

Selling to your boss requires careful consideration. Don't forget he is more powerful. Make use of the basic Five Dimensional Management rules, including the use of trusted colleagues and friends. It's your decision as to what to do but counselling a colleague is often of benefit.

Another situation may be where there is no such problem, but you simply want something that is of obvious benefit to you although the benefits are not so obvious to anyone else.

Why should the boss want to let you have or do something like this? Unless he is a Democrat and just likes saying yes, you may be rejected; if so, however unreasonable the request was, you will feel a bit upset.

When making any such proposal, you probably will only be able to persuade the boss if there is a genuine benefit to others or the business. So you have to find out and point out these benefits, or trade what you want for something equally of benefit to others or the business.

As a simple example, if you wanted to go to college to study a foreign language one night a week, your boss may agree to pay for it if you spend a lunchtime each week training the new junior secretary on how to use the latest word-processing package. Don't be shy in making such proposals, but always ensure as much as you can that the boss will see the benefit to the business, otherwise you will be accused of being self-centred and greedy - even if you're not.

5. *Measuring – the boss*
To determine how effective you are as a 5DM manager.

How to measure how good you are at managing your boss.

As mentioned earlier, measuring management capability is to a degree subjective. This does not mean it should not be done. It should be done all the time. If we do not know or admit where we need training, then we won't get it and can't benefit from it.

The method of measuring we recommend is to go back to the skills list and ask a number of people to score or rank your management capability in those areas. You should at least ask your boss, three or four colleagues and hopefully two or three other people. Peers of your boss are a good idea, as they may have a say when it comes to you being promoted. You should also fill the form in yourself and see if your view of yourself is similar to that of your colleagues.

One way of ensuring honesty is to organise it so that the forms do not have a name on. You can design the forms yourself, but the following is an example of a simple one that has been used successfully.

Your name is: **Boss is "............................"**

Please take two minutes to help determine how successful she/he is at managing 'the boss'.

Please tick the appropriate number.
"1" for No or very poor   "6" for Yes or very very good

No   Yes
1 2 3 4 5 6

1. Do you think - 'you' - is a good communicator?

2. Do you think s/he has good verbal skills?

3. Do you think s/he communicates well with the boss?

4. Do you think s/he helps the boss in doing his/her job?

5. Do you think the boss feels appreciated?

6. Do you think s/he wastes the boss' time?

7. Do you think s/he is a good organiser?

8. Does s/he try to persuade the boss to do things well?

9. Does s/he know the boss?

10. Does s/he know the boss' objectives?

Do not be disappointed that people consider you have strengths and weaknesses. Don't believe it if they say you are wonderful at everything. Compare it to your own view of your performance. Equally, don't believe it if they say you are hopeless at everything.

The only person who will have access to all the information

is you, so everyone can afford to be honest. Only by receiving honest comments can you grow.

Depending upon the situation we believe it is a good idea to carry out this type of exercise about once a year.

Managing in all your dimensions is important. Possibly managing the boss is the most difficult. Many people will not have viewed their boss in this way ever before. Some bosses will not like it. The better ones will encourage it. You don't need anyone's permission to be a Five Dimensional Manager.

SUMMARY OF CHAPTER FOUR

Managing The Boss

1. Get to know your boss, his/her strengths and weaknesses.

2. Find out what his/her objectives are - personal and business.

3. Be as intelligent as you can be as to how you manage your boss as he/she probably has more information and hence more power than you.

4. Your boss is not and cannot be a threat to you in the medium or long term in terms of you eventually fulfilling your potential. If you believe he or she is, it's your responsibility.

5. Your boss needs appropriate and sincere praise.

CHAPTER 5

The 2nd Dimension - Managing Internal Colleagues And Peers

How do you get co-operation from people over whom you have no authority and who do not have any formal responsibility to help you? This category includes people in different departments, different buildings, different locations. It includes people whose job may seem to conflict with yours.

What's in it for them? What's in it for you?

Five Dimensional Management is to do with appreciating other people, their roles and how they all link together. It is easy to say it's nothing to do with you. It's easy to criticise someone for the way they do their job. But neither attitude is helpful and neither is good management. To be a manager and to move up the management ladder, even just one rung, we have to understand what it is that the other people do.

To be a Five Dimensional Manager you have to start from the basis that everyone prefers to do a good job and that everyone's job is worthwhile. This is very important.

There have been numerous studies proving that successful companies employ better people and that better people earn more and achieve more within those companies. If your company, even your department, does better than expected then you will be perceived as being a part of that success. You will have made a contribution. You will have been noticed. In addition you will feel good about yourself, you will have made a step towards being fulfilled.

You will also have gained knowledge about your department, other departments, other people's jobs, other people and about management.

And if you do help someone, if you do try to make things better, there is no downside. Even if it does not work out exactly as you had planned, if done intelligently and with consideration you can only win. The potential benefits are considerable, the downside is nil. And on top of all that you may be amazed at which people start helping you.

Before going into the basic 5DM management techniques, remember that you need to know the individual who you are managing. Is she autocratic; if so what do you do? Is he a bubbly extrovert, if so what do you do? Is she the sort of person who needs constant reassurance?

Remember the 5DM Golden Rule: "Manage them the way they need to be managed".

Remember, we do not say the way they want to be managed. Good managers definitely do not just do what other people want them to do. That is not management.

Arrange so that you can spend some time with a colleague you deal with in another department or office with whom there is a problem. Tell them the purpose of the meeting is to try to help them by making their job easier. The format of the meeting can be varied to suit the circumstances and personalities involved. However, an idea in this regard is to have a four step approach.

First, ask them to tell you about their job and what their department/office does. Listen carefully. Do not assume that you know. It's a funny thing but people like to be listened to when they are talking. As they talk ask questions on any point you do not fully understand. They may assume that you understand something you do not. By asking such questions you are creating the right mood for the meeting i.e. you are there to learn.

Second, explain what you do, with particular emphasis upon where your two departments/offices come into contact.

Third, ask how you or your department can make their job easier. If any problems they have were not mentioned during the first stage, then ask what they are now . When you know them write down 20 options together and together make a conscious decision. Don't forget, for the idea to work it may well be that the other person has to have the final word - so that they 'own' the decision. Equally it may be that you are entitled to make that final decision.

The fourth phase is 'Any Other Business' - whatever comes up in conversation. The other person may want to discuss something else, although if this was the case your approach hopefully would have been flexible enough to have allowed any pressing issues to have been raised. In turn, you may respect the person, so you want to ask their advice as to another problem you have.

At this point you have still not stated the specific problems you have with the other department/office. But you may do so now, or not, as you feel appropriate. As with all things judgement is required. Some people will be wary and think that the whole purpose of the meeting was for you to get them to do something for you. It would be far better to have a vastly improved working relationship than to spoil it by asking for help too soon.

The whole approach is to be positive, constructive, motivational and of obvious benefit to both parties.

What happens if the other person does not have any problems and - to create a worse case situation - you cannot or do not wish to mention any? Explain to the person that you believe that things can always be improved on the basis that things are always changing. Say that, having explained to them what you do, you would like their help as to how what you do could be improved. Try to get the two of you to come up with 20 ideas and then, together, choose two or three that you are going to implement. Most people will be flattered to have been asked. Most people will be able to make a contribution.

Having decided on two or three things to implement (too many at any one time may well be a mistake), you then have to agree how to bring about the changes. If they are minor ones then you can probably just get on with them. If not, you may have to get the co-operation or permission of others, possibly the boss. How you communicate such ideas should become apparent as you read through this book.

1. *Communication - with internal colleagues*
   Getting the right message to the right person at the right time in the right way to get the right results.

In many companies, conversations between colleagues revolve around carrying out their respective tasks, social matters and office gossip. We are suggesting that you add a fourth. A regular, possibly monthly or three monthly meeting of no more than half an hour (the first one may have to be an hour) to brain storm as to how things can be improved. How can you help each other?

Speaking to each other is, of course, only one way of communicating; as with all other people you are managing, you need to be aware of all the other methods of communicating and the relative importance of each.

Written communication is sometimes a good idea. Many people rightly believe we create too much paperwork, so use your judgement. But don't just put in writing official memos that need be recorded. Also, tell everyone of some good work that a colleague has done, of an internal promotion, of a good idea that has been implemented.

Body language is also important and not just for people working in reception. What you wear, how you speak, the length of your hair are all statements you make. If everyone in your company dresses casually and you continually come to work in a grey three-piece suit with tie, realise what you're communicating.

The opposite is also true. Not that you have to lose your individuality, but we all work better with people who fit into the same broad culture.

How you speak, your vocabulary, your use of bad language; these are all examples of communication and they are all messages that you give so that your colleagues know how to manage you. Make your decisions about such things consciously, make them all positive.

2. *Motivation - of your internal colleagues*
The process by which someone does something because they want to.

As with the other sections how you motivate your colleagues can come in various forms. Many of them will be motivated by the justified praise they receive for doing their job well. Others will be motivated by being asked their opinion. Others by being a recognisable part of a successful team.

The definition recognises that people are self motivated but perform at their best in the most conducive environment. So the question is how can you improve the working environment of your colleagues? Obviously there are innumerable ways - and far more than 20. Many of them are such that the conscious decisions technique can be used, others will happen on a more day to day basis.

The personnel director of a large British construction company was asked to convene a meeting between two of his fellow directors. Both were very experienced men, highly forceful, and they had a major disagreement as to an important policy matter that had to be resolved.

At the meeting things quickly became very heated as their predetermined, entrenched positions were restated. Despite the personnel director's best efforts, the discussions escalated to the extent whereby one of the directors felt he had no option but to storm out of the room.

The remaining director asked the personnel man what was to happen now. The personnel director replied that he felt the man remaining had to go and find the colleague who had stormed out and apologise to him. The director who was also quite heated, replied in no uncertain terms that he did not feel that it was he who should be apologising. The personnel director disagreed. Eventually the colleague remaining went to find the director who had left. Having done so, he said, "Fred, I want to apologise. I don't know what I did to make you storm out like that, but whatever it was, that was not my intention. Why don't you come back because whatever happens we have to agree as to what we are going to do".

That apology, a sincere one and the words he used were solely his, totally defused the situation. The other director apologised for storming out, they returned and eventually reached an agreement. Even better, after that they worked together on an improved basis. The environment was such they now wanted to work together. They were both motivated to do so.

Another story told by the same personnel director, one of the best examples of natural Five Dimensional Management we have met, is as follows:

He went to a construction site to 'deliver' a young graduate who had joined the company that day. The site was a bit off the beaten track and thus was not visited as often by directors as maybe it should have been. On the way there, the personnel director had continued the induction discussion by confirming the company's commitment to quality, training etc.

Upon arrival, they walked into the site offices to meet the manager - only to find the offices in an absolutely disgraceful state of untidiness. They were filthy. Realising the effect that this would have upon the young graduate, the director felt he had to do something immediately.

He told the manager that, coincidentally, the owner of the company was in the area and planning to drop by for a surprise visit. The manager was terrified. Within minutes four or five men, plus the graduate and the personnel director were cleaning, washing up, sweeping and putting things away. After an hour the place had been transformed. Then they all rushed into the temporary car park and picked up milk bottles, waste paper etc, eventually returning to the office with the site manager muttering how grateful he was that he had been tipped off and that the owner had not yet arrived.

It was then that the personnel director told him the owner was not coming. They had a discussion, with the graduate in attendance, with the site manager doing most of the talking. He knew he was in the wrong and he knew why he had been told the white lie. No criticism or further comments were necessary from the director.

Motivation comes in many forms. The personnel director in that story knew it was no good telling the site manager to tidy up his office. The site manager had to want to keep it tidy. He had to realise it was in his interest and in everyone else's that he did so.

To motivate your colleagues to perform better and/or help you and other colleagues, you have to create an environment whereby they want to do better. Whereby they will be motivated to sustain an improved level of performance.

It is never, or very rarely, down to money, despite what some people may tell you. Money only achieves a short term gain.

Praise, training, variety of task - all these are examples of how you can motivate your colleagues.

3. *Planning - internal colleagues*
   Determining the most effective way of co-ordinating and actioning those resources needed to complete a task.

To manage your colleagues through planning may involve reverting back to managing their time in one or more of several ways.

If you can save your colleague some time, i.e. make them more efficient, then that is one way. Alternatively, if you can assist them in being better time managers then that is another. Most people need some improvement in this area and most need reminding of time management.

One of the problems you have in this regard is how to get the message through to a colleague - someone over whom you have no authority - that you want to help their time management. If you just tell them they are likely to resent the idea.

Again the answer can be found in one of the Five Dimensional Management basic principles. Ask questions, ask for their help. It may be that you could go to the colleague, say that it is sometime since you reviewed your time management and you would like to know how they do it. What advice can they give you? Ask to have 15 minutes with them in a few days' time. This will give them time to give the matter some thought and to put their own house in order.

By making use of the 20 options technique, you will be able to write down some of the other person's good ideas. You will almost certainly gain from the experience; so will your colleague.

He or she may well admit they are not good at it or need improvement, in which case you can say that you are the same and why don't the two of you spend the 15 minutes brain storming to come up with a couple of ideas that you will both then use? Let your colleague suggest ideas to use. At the end of the meeting, thank them for their help - assuming they have been of some help, which is almost certainly the case.

That's only one idea. Another is to help them with organisation resources. A young lady was explaining to a colleague that she spent all day, everyday, ringing up stationery suppliers getting prices for future orders in accordance with company instructions. The problem was that telephones were engaged, the right person was not there, they could not give a price straightaway over the 'phone etc. The colleague suggested they had lunch together and try to come up with some answers to the problem.

Over lunch with both of them having had some time to think about the problem, they came up with 20 options. The young lady with the problem chose one of them. She chose to fax five companies on a standard form asking them for their price and date of delivery if an order was placed. She was delighted to be off the 'phone. The company saved money, the girl had time to do other things, the prices were confirmed in writing and the stationery companies perceived it as a serious enquiry, rather than someone just ringing round. Everyone benefited. The colleague suggested that the girl ask to go on a Five Dimensional Management seminar as a reward.

4. *Sell - to internal colleagues*
To motivate someone to buy an idea, product or services that they want.

Selling is persuading. Being sold to is being persuaded. If you are prepared to listen, prepared to learn then you can be persuaded. And only if you learn will you grow.

If you or your colleagues are intransigent or 'know it alls', then you will not change and you are not a manager. You cannot be a manager if you do not change to reflect the constantly changing environment that we live in and the constantly changing people that it comprises.

Persuading does not mean getting your own way and it does not mean getting someone to 'buy' something that they do not want.

Persuading is to do with providing someone with additional information - facts not opinions - thus making them realise they need to change something.

If you believe that a colleague needs to change something they do, it may be appropriate that you point out his/her problems with the normal methods and solutions to the problem. It may be that when you raise the problem together you come up with 20 options. Obviously your preferred option will possibly gain more attention in terms of justification. But remember, if the person feels you only really have one option that you are considering he or she may feel pressurised and create resistance to it.

When persuading anyone and especially someone from another department who has a different boss to you, you have to show judgement. You may not fully appreciate all the facts of the situation. You may be wrong. As a rule of thumb when persuading, you should listen at least as much as you talk.

5. *Measuring - internal colleagues*
To determine how effective you are as a 5DM manager.

How to measure how good you are at managing your colleagues.

Using the normal approach to measuring you ask them to fill in a questionnaire that you give them. We always recommend they leave their names off it so that you can obtain their honest opinions. If necessary, do it through a third party. Invite, say six colleagues from varying departments or offices. Also ask one or two others for their opinions.

Again the questions showed revolve around the five management skills. The other suggested questionnaires in the book will help you evolve your own questionnaire but on the next page you will find a suggested format. As usual, also fill the form in yourself so that you can determine whether your self perception is similar to that of others.

'Your' Name

In terms of managing or getting on with 'his' colleagues, please take a few minutes to answer the following questions.

Put a tick against the appropriate number.
"1" for No or very poor   "6" for Yes or very very good

	No	Yes
	1 2 3	4 5 6

1. Is he good at verbal communication?

2. Is he good at other forms of communication?

3. Does he dress appropriately?

4. Is he persuasive?

5. Is he helpful?

6. Is he a good organiser?

7. Is he tidy?

8. Is he objective?

9. Does he say thank you?

Other relevant comments as to his management abilities:

Remember the purpose of the exercise is not to allow people the opportunity of criticising you. It is to obtain their opinions of your strengths and weaknesses, to compare their opinions to yours and to identify those areas where improvement is required.

The very best sportsmen in the world receive tuition virtually all the time. The very best operatic singers do likewise. Managers are no different. To admit that we have strengths and weaknesses does not mean that we are not valuable, important and capable. It means that we want to improve.

SUMMARY OF CHAPTER FIVE

Managing Internal Colleagues

1. All your internal colleagues can influence your success or otherwise and vice versa.

2. By learning more about what they do you will become more promotable.

3. Managed correctly most of your colleagues will help you be a better manager.

4. Listen more carefully. Listening means learning, means growing, means Don't Make Assumptions.

CHAPTER 6

The 3rd Dimension - Managing External Colleagues

As described earlier, this dimension of people is crucial to many businesses and yet very few of them are managed as we believe they should be. An 'us and them' situation has been created, again probably for perfectly reasonable historical reasons. But not to consciously manage them is an error. To treat them well, to manage them well is in everybody's interest. Of course, many of them have to be competitive, commercial and to deliver on time but by managing them well all this and more will be achieved.

How are we going to manage those people with whom we have no direct relationship, with whom we have little control direct or otherwise and who are inevitably based in a different location, possibly overseas?

Accepting they are important and therefore need managing does not necessarily tell us enough about why we need to manage them. What are the benefits for us and for the external colleague we are managing?

The first benefit, again common to all the other dimensions, is that we can improve our management skills and hence move up the management ladder quicker. Also by getting to know the individuals, what they do and their problems, we enhance our knowledge and experience.

There are other, possibly less obvious, benefits. Many of them can make us more effective, more successful by giving us a better, quicker service. Many of them, by word of mouth, could get us business, or recommend us as an employer. When you really have a serious problem and need help - perhaps overnight - your management of them might be the deciding factor.

Again, in common with much of Five Dimensional Management, what is the downside? What can go wrong in you managing your external colleagues in an intelligent, conscious and considerate way?

To achieve these benefits and others we revert to the 5DM skills.

1. *Communication - with external colleagues*
   Getting the right message to the right person at the right time in the right way to get the right results.

Very often there is considerably less personal contact than normal with external colleagues, with more of it being by telephone and in writing. With less information to work with even greater attention needs to be given to the information at your disposal in an effort to get to know the person you are managing.

It may be a good idea to invite the person to visit your office or place of work to walk round and meet everyone. Why not invite your office cleaner, who usually attends your office out of normal hours, to meet everyone?

There was once a cleaner who had the initiative to answer a ringing telephone, having been taught how to use the switchboard. She took a call from an overseas customer that resulted in a £multi-million order. If you communicated better with your cleaner, a similar benefit might come about for you.

Dealing with people on the telephone is an everyday occurrence nowadays. Because of this, hopefully we have become better at 'reading' such people.

If you think of these people on the telephone as people you should be managing, what does it mean if they talk very quickly? What does it mean if they talk slowly? What does it mean if they talk slowly about their caravan as opposed to talking slowly about small business-related details? What types of people are they? Are you consciously managing these people differently?

Are you doing it sub-consciously?

When next talking to these external colleagues, try to write down what sort of person they are and then write down how best to manage them and how best to communicate with them. When writing down what sort of person they are we do not mean physically but in terms of personality, intellect and experience. Think about how you are going to determine each of these. If you find it difficult ask for someone's help. Only by doing so can you communicate effectively; by that we mean effectively for both of you.

When communicating with customers, very often there is a further complication. Very often the main problem is how and what to communicate without just saying, "Have you got any orders?". There are many things that can be done and in some instances, in some industries, certain companies are excellent at this.

One of the more obvious examples of this is to keep customers fully informed as to how their current orders are proceeding. As an extreme example, you should not be too concerned with telling them you are overcoming problems. There is a balance to be struck so as to allow them to manage foreseeable, inevitable delays. Judgement is required and with this everybody gets it wrong sometimes. With intelligent judgement most customers prefer to be told too early rather than too late. You may decide to involve your boss before giving really bad news. If for no other reason than he or she will want to be kept informed and may have a solution to the problem. (Although hopefully you will have 'managed' that before alerting the customer).

Other methods of communicating include writing, other than just the necessary items. Also: inter-company social functions, an external colleague of the month competition, sending your external colleagues a copy of your company's newsletter in return for one of theirs, combining your Christmas parties, asking for their help. The list is endless.

2. *Motivation - of external colleagues*
   The process by which someone does something because they want to.

To motivate external colleagues is to create a situation whereby they want to do their best for you.

One of the obvious ways to motivate a supplier is to let them know that a good performance will be given proper consideration when forthcoming orders are placed. You might be able to tell them that another order will be let shortly or that you can influence how soon they get paid.

Two items of warning. Never make promises you cannot keep; most people will give you one chance, but rarely a second.

Second, never just give people new orders without going through the proper procedures. In extreme cases and if you really have to, only do so with the written approval of your boss.

Most people are motivated to work and do their best for well run, well managed businesses. If you show them that you are not a well run business, 'human nature' may take over leading to the inevitable decline in their performance.

Another obvious way to motivate external colleagues to do their best for you, is to do your best for them and that includes doing them 'favours'. Not anything that in anyway compromises you or your company; that is not a favour, that's called stupidity. But for example, if a supplier is unable to deliver the components on time, check if you still need them all on the due date. Possibly your production has slipped or your client could wait without causing any hardship.

If you try to be constructive rather than invoking the penalty clause, it is a sure thing they will help you the next time. And what's the downside?

For you there are also other benefits in managing these colleagues well. They can provide you with useful information. Such as what your competitors are doing, new developments in the market, other markets you could get into, the first option on a new component being launched. The possibilities are endless. All as a result of good management and motivated colleagues.

3. *Planning - external colleagues*
Determining the most effective way of co-ordinating and actioning those resources needed to complete a task.

The planning of external colleagues is again an unusual concept in the traditional way of considering management. And again it cannot be looked at in isolation to all the other Five Dimensional Management skills.

They are all inter-related. How to assist your external colleagues plan better falls into two areas, broadly speaking. First, provide them with information and obtain information from them so that you can both do better planning. The success of good planning relies upon the quality of information available.

Second, communicate with the person on how you both do your planning and about problems you both have in doing it. If you have such an exchange and if you ask his/her advice, who knows what might happen? At the very least you will know how good you are at planning. At best you might be able to initiate a great improvement and have a highly motivated supplier, one who feels a part of the team as opposed to one who feels unimportant. If you're going to work with these people you might as well get the best out of them and give of your very best to them.

What about planning other, more difficult, external colleagues? Let us choose the customer, the person we want business from. Again, this can be done on several different levels.

One option is to inform your customer how you do your planning in your company. What improvements you have brought about since the last time. Ask for their opinions on an important issue. Conduct a survey. Relatively few companies undertake proper research to determine such matters, instead tending to rely on hearsay and subjectivity.

Another option is to ask them how they do their planning, so that you can fit into their systems better when future orders come about. Ask what problems they have experienced in planning when orders are placed.

Instead of constantly badgering your customers for future orders, why not agree a rota when contact should be made - on the basis that if anything happened in the meantime they would let you know. At the same time always ask who else within their company you should be keeping in contact with. Most people appreciate a constructive attempt at resolving an issue. You might stop wasting time making abortive 'phone calls and do something useful. In some businesses this could work, in others it wouldn't. Use your judgement, use your intelligence, manage by making conscious decisions.

In some instances and in some industries, management is quite sophisticated. But for most of us there is almost certainly room for improvement. However, it may not be your responsibility for such matters. You may not be the person given the responsibility although you do have contact with the relevant external colleagues.

Much of pre 5DM or traditional management was based upon a 'need to know' basis. In other words, do not give information unless they need it. In 5DM we work from the other extreme. Most information can be given without there being any problem and most of the remainder can be entrusted to people that you know well. In addition, the motivational effect is considerable. Most people respond well to being trusted and they will trust you.

There are, of course, any number of ways the 5DM skills can be used. In terms of planning or working together, assuming that you are not the person responsible, it may well be that keeping your external colleagues informed is all that you can do. By doing so you might be able to ask for their advice. Almost certainly they will keep you better informed and they might ask your advice.

With the knowledge of the person responsible you might be able to act as a mediator, an informal message giver and receiver.

If you appreciate their problems better, and they yours, things can only improve.

4. *Sell - to external colleagues*
To motivate someone to buy an idea, product or services that they want.

Dealing with customers is an immense subject. Many books have been written on this one topic. A few of them are worth reading. In Britain as a whole and certainly amongst such sectors as building/civil contractors, privatised industries and service companies, the salesmanship is, as a generalisation, abysmal. The main reason being that they do not know what is possible. Also, to justify their performance to-date, they refuse to learn and change. The justification is always that their industry is unique and hence so are their problems.

There are a few basics that must be adhered to when dealing with customers.

1. Know your marketplace. Know who your competitors are, where they are strong, where they are weak; know where they are better than you, where they are weaker. Get to know their pricing policy. To obtain this information proper research should be done.

2. You should also know your key customers' potential and existing budgets. Their long term plans, strategies. Again research should be done.

3. Get to know the key individuals, the decision makers. Literally get to know what they drink, where they live, where they go on holiday, how old the kids are. Not that you should necessarily bring these things up in conversation, but for two other reasons you should be aware:

a) The more you know the person the more relaxed you will be when dealing with them.

b) Only by knowing them can you determine whether or not you are the person who should try to get business from them. Or, put another way, whether or not you are the person who should mange them.

4. Know your business. It sounds obvious, but many people don't. If you only sell roof tiles and not bricks, and both are products of your company, you should know all about bricks. The person who buys roof tiles probably buys bricks as well. And if not they know who in their company does.

5. Be able to talk in detail of the history of your company, the background of the directors. Know your company's financial standing and the group's, in terms of, at the very least, turnover and profit.

Whether you like it or not, people are going to buy what you are selling based upon you. The more credible and therefore reliable you are, the better your chance of success.

In many instances (again the industries mentioned earlier spring to mind) a tremendous opportunity exists for an individual to show some initiative so that their company is known to be head and shoulders better than their competitors. For example, one could suggest setting up an induction programme and making all the information available to all their salespeople, i.e everyone. Many companies do not have a formal induction programme. Not even for their sales staff.

As to other external colleagues, the opportunity to sell is not so obvious until we remind ourselves that selling is the provision of information to allow people to make better quality buying decisions. This includes the buying of an idea to do something differently.

If you see someone doing something which you believe could be done better, you have a management responsibility to do something about it. But lots of judgement is required. First, this must not be done at the expense of the job you are paid to do. Second, if done badly the colleague in question can take offence and that will be your responsibility.

To try to sell to a willing listener can be difficult. To try to sell to someone who does not want to listen is virtually impossible and may even have negative repercussions.

Your approach must depend entirely upon your relationship with the person in question. The more you know the person, the better; if you like each other; better still, but even then care has to be taken. You could be wrong about the whole thing.

The 5DM approach to all such matters is to begin by *asking* questions. You might start as gently as possible by saying as little as "How is it going?" before gradually becoming more specific. Often a rehearsal is required before you will feel ready to do this, even if it is on the telephone. If the topic you wish to discuss is not forthcoming from your colleague you then have to be bolder but more careful. You might try saying "How is the invoicing going?" (or whatever topic it is you had in mind) "You seemed to be saying the other day that you were having problems".

Or you could say, "I was talking to a colleague about invoicing recently and they do something that might be of interest".

What you must not do is act as a 'know it all' - because you don't. Equally you must not be seen to be criticising as you do not know all the facts. These people do not even work for your company, let alone report to you.

As soon as the topic is out in the open you can get them to say what the problem is; then you can discuss solutions, including the one you have in mind and the justification. And there you have to stop. You cannot do any more. It would be improper and arrogant to suggest your solution or any other as being the best one.

If you can (providing it is true), you should end positively by saying something like how you felt the discussion was very worthwhile and perhaps you could have another chat when you have a problem.

When anyone from any dimension asks for your advice you should never assume you know best, that you know the solution. Even then, even if you arrogantly did, the challenge would be to get them to realise the solution for themselves without you telling them, so that they 'own' the solution.

6. *Measuring - external colleagues*
To determine how effective you are as a 5DM manager.

Using the now familiar Five Dimensional Management concept, we ask people for their opinions. We obtain an average on each item and then compare it to our own view of our management capability.

Again we design the questionnaires; again it may be better if you have them completed anonymously and/or through a third party.

When undertaking any such measuring a short explanation may be necessary. Internal, let alone external, colleagues, particularly at a more junior level, may find it unusual to be asked opinions of someone's management abilities. This does not invalidate their opinions and it is a part of their management development.

Although everyone is encouraged to prepare their own questionnaires, there are various principles we recommend:

1. They should not take more than two or three minutes to complete and therefore tick boxes are encouraged wherever possible. Also, in measuring management skills no more than eight or 10 questions should ever be required.

2. When asking people to give a score don't let them have a middle number to tick. Often people tick the middle one as opposed to expressing an opinion or giving the matter due consideration. Ranking is another good idea. This is where they rank the management skills you list in order of your ability.

3. Keep it simple.

4. When looking at the results, if all the questions are scored the same disregard them all. Irrespective of how flattering or otherwise they may be.

When determining your management skills of external colleagues, choose a spectrum of people. Choose different types of external colleagues: one or two suppliers, one or two customers and possibly one or two others. Also give the questionnaire to your boss or an internal colleague who also deals with the same external people. Ensure that you obtain a valid concensus so that you can obtain a meaningful measure of your current abilities.

A suggested questionnaire:

We are trying to determine the development of 'you' in terms of their man-management ability. As a valued external colleague would you mind completing this form and returning it to us. Hopefully this will lead to an even better relationship in the future.

For each question please tick one number.

"1" is No or bad   "6" is Yes or exceptionally good

No   Yes
1 2 3 4 5 6

1. Does she speak clearly and effectively?

2. Does she write clearly and effectively?

3. Does she listen well?

4. Is she generally helpful?

5. Would you ask her advice regarding a
   related problem?

6. Is she well organised?

7. Is her work accurate?

8. Is she persuasive?

9. Does she say thank you?

Other relevant comments:

SUMMARY OF CHAPTER SIX

Managing External Colleagues

1. External colleagues are essential to your business, to you and your managerial future.

2. Of all these important people customers are the most important and need the most careful consideration.

3. You will never know as much about their business and their problems as they do.

4. Even if you did, you should never tell them where they are going wrong. Not even when asked to do so.

CHAPTER 7

The 4th Dimension - Managing Subordinates

T oday's younger subordinates are better educated, more mature and have been brought up in a fast-moving, more materialistic society of computers, fast cars and holidays abroad. They also enter their working life just as inexperienced and just as optimistic as we did. Hopefully.

A great deal can be learnt from subordinates, especially those younger than ourselves. They all have different experiences, they all have different needs. We need to learn as much from them as we can.

In terms of man-management, subordinates should hardly ever be told what to do and how to do it. They should have tasks, responsibilities and goals to achieve. And they should know what quality is required, what timescale is permissable and in both cases why. They should also be told how well they have done and be given praise as often as is genuinely deserved. As should everybody else.

If they are continually told what to do or what the solution to the problem is, they will never learn to think for themselves. They will never make mistakes, they will assume you know best - and you don't. If you tell them what to do all the time or if you continually criticise then eventually they will resent it and they will not come to you with their problems. Then you're really in trouble because they have information that you need to know.

Subordinates are entitled to certain things just as much as we all are. The main one being that, as a boss, you have to see to it that the person grows, develops, learns and leaves the experience enriched with new found skills. Those skills might be managerial, technical, (eg, knowledge of a new word processing package) or derived from study at night school. Thus, not even necessarily obviously relevant. By broadening the person's experience, he/she will be a better and more motivated person. Such people perform better at work.

Many people will find some of those statements quite contentious. Let's try to pre-empt some of their criticisms. Sometimes, although rarely, people do have to be told what to do. Including us, as bosses. But not often. Normally we are reasonable and we can be persuaded. Normally we are intelligent and if not threatened can learn from our mistakes.

Also, there is only so much one can do for an individual because of various constraints such as money, time, getting the job done and the motivation of the subordinate in question. Yet even when the person says they do not want to be developed, it is still the responsibility of the boss to do so.

Another thing that a subordinate is entitled to is loyalty from the boss.

A boss should not expect a subordinate to be as good as he is in every aspect. Now and again a subordinate may be, they may be better in many aspects but often do not have as much information as the boss.

A subordinate is entitled to honesty from his/her boss. Indeed it could be argued that everyone is entitled to honesty from everyone else. However, that would be idealistic and ignores conflicts of interests. Bosses should have the same business interests as subordinates. Subordinates are entitled to look to their bosses to learn that honesty and openness are the way forward. Lies and deceit cause irrevocable decay.

Whilst looking at managing subordinates through the Five

Dimensional Management skills and philosophy, it should also be remembered that the boss' management skills are a key way but not the only way to develop the subordinate's management skills. It is, therefore, necessary for the boss to sometimes explain the technique in more detail as well as the normal discussion and justifications.

Another general point that should be made about Five Dimensional Management is that many people have in the past found it easier and quicker not to go to all this trouble. It's easier just to tell them what to do.

This is very short term thinking. The development of people and businesses is a long term, indeed never ending, project. Autocracy can work in the short term but not in the long term unless you are exceptionally intelligent and talented. And most of us are far from that.

Also remember that people cannot learn to become good managers or to change established management habits quickly. Indeed, regarding this latter point it is often unwise to change established practices quickly as this can trivialise the subject or make it appear insincere.

1. *Communication - with subordinates*
   Getting the right message to the right person at the right time in the right way to get the right results.

When communicating with subordinates it should always be remembered that in all probability they will look at you, the boss, in a totally different way to how you see yourself.

You may well see yourself as a reasonable, intelligent, democratic, humorous person. They could see you as being unreasonable, undemocratic, serious and threatening. To be able to receive the correct messages or communications, credibility has to be established. This often means consistency. Not that anyone should believe they can be perfect or are consistent all the time. As a boss you can be human and that includes making mistakes. But when you do make a mistake, admit it, apologise and point out the solution. The worst of bosses have one set of rules for themselves and another for subordinates. The worst of bosses would never apologise if ever they made a mistake but then they would reckon they never do anyway. These people justify and cover up their mistakes rather than say sorry. By being honest the boss will enable his subordinates to do the same. But if he behaves badly, subordinates will come to believe that this is the way up the management ladder.

The methods of communication are the same as ever: speaking, writing, informal meetings, formal meetings, one to one chats, vocabulary, body language, dress etc.

Different bosses have different preferred methods. Within Five Dimensional Management we have certain preferences but the best method often depends upon the personalities and the situation at hand.

Informal speaking on a one to one basis whenever possible is recommended. The reasons include: the subordinate gets 100% attention even if it's only for a short time; the subordinate will also receive the management appropriate to them whereas in a group the problem is more complex; and most people find that honesty is easier - for both parties - on a one to one basis.

Meetings both formal and informal have to be held, but in our opinion as infrequently as possible. The justification for this attitude includes:

1. Some people get upset if they feel excluded.

2. Others have to be invited but play no part.

3. They nearly always take too long. (If you perceive this as a problem don't have comfortable chairs or better still don't have chairs at all!).

4. Minutes have to be taken; this involves time and often is not necessary. As a generalisation when minutes are

required, they should only record decisions taken and not an account of the discussions that took place to reach the decision.

When mistakes are made or when a reprimand is required, this should always be done in private and on a one to one basis. It goes without saying that ideally the boss should not lose his temper but if it does happen the quicker the apology is delivered the better. If a reprimand is erroneously delivered in front of others then so should the apology.

At the beginning of the chapter it was stated that bosses should hardly ever tell subordinates what to do. To many bosses, especially autocratic ones or ones with ego problems, that is almost their sole function. So how does a new 5DM boss communicate in this situation, one in which he or she is in the habit of giving the answer?

As an example, if a subordinate has a problem, he or she should seek approval for a chosen solution but should not expect or receive a solution from the boss.

In this instance, the subordinate should state the problem. The boss should then ask for the options being considered to resolve the situation. If the boss thinks that he knows the answer and if it is not included in the options then he can try to get it from the subordinate by asking questions. If that does not work then the boss can suggest other options, including the preferred one, giving each of them equal emphasis and justification. The boss should then allow the subordinate to choose the preferred solution. In most cases this method will provide an agreeable solution.

Sometimes when this procedure is explained people think it will take too long or that it's unnecessary or that the wrong solution will be chosen. Try it, trust it.

If, as a boss, you are absolutely certain that the chosen solution is horribly wrong you will have no problem in quickly demonstrating this and doing so without undermining the subordinate's self-esteem. The reason is nearly always that they did not have all the facts.

Remember, people will not come to the boss with problems without solutions once they have confidence in their own abilities and once they know what is required of them. Remember that the subordinate is intelligent, wants to do a good job and often knows the problem better than the boss. Remember that if they make the decision not only do they learn better but they are more likely to make it work. Remember that even when bosses 'know' the answer they can be wrong.

Subordinates will only develop, so that you the boss can be promoted, if they are allowed to make decisions. If you make their decisions for them you may make yourself indispensable so that you cannot be promoted; then you will definitely not retain and get the best out of quality subordinates.

In one particular company two senior managers were both hoping to be promoted as the next production director. In many ways the two people were very similar. Both were equally successful. One of them worked tremendously hard, was constantly on the go, sorting out problems, attending meetings and writing reports. The other was hardly ever busy, he always had time. He seemed to manage by walking around and having the odd word with his staff. The first one could not believe it when the "lazy so and so" got the promotion. He had made himself indispensable so that his team could not operate without him. The second person had prepared himself and his team for the situation.

2. *Motivation - of subordinates*
The process by which someone does something because they want to.

The first, most obvious motivator is praise. Regretfully, it is not used often enough, often leading to a cynical attitude when it is.

Praise has to be sincere and justified, and it does not have to be for major achievements only. Praise can come in a number of ways, verbal being the first that would spring to most people's mind. But although highly recommended, verbal praise needs some thought and is not the only method available.

A few words of congratulation on a one to one basis is very different to similar words in front of colleagues. This again would be different if carried out informally as opposed to formally. All these methods and others should be used on occasions.

Other ways of saying well done include a memo or letter copied to other people in the organisation. The company newsletter, the noticeboard, the electronic diary system. Giving a bunch of flowers, a book, a dinner for him/her and spouse. All ways should be considered and used as appropriate. Praise should not be predictable.

Most people respond well to praise and public acknowledgement.

But not all. How do you praise good old Fred, Fred the Dependable, the quiet, introvert who goes about his work in an unassuming way and who is essential to the smooth running of the factory? That is the challenge to a good boss. Ignore Fred at your peril. And don't think you can just give him more money. In fact, as a generalisation, do not think that money alone will motivate anyone. Not even if they tell you that money is exactly what they want.

Motivation revolves around, once again, getting to know the individual and working out what he or she wants, what makes them tick.

One boss had a perfectly competent secretary, one who he was quite happy with. The only problem he had was that she would not take any initiative. She would not positively help him and hence she was not using all her skills. She was in her early 50s, quite old for this particular company, and prior to joining it (nine months earlier) had been out of work for several months. As she lived on her own, she had not enjoyed this enforced 'holiday' as it had caused an amount of financial pressure.

During a discussion and by asking questions, the boss realised that she was worried about losing her job and that by not showing any initiative she felt she was safer and less likely to be made redundant.

Our hero, the 5DM boss then considered various options and her performance to date. He called her into his office and said (again) that he thought her work was, in general, excellent but that she was capable of more.

The two of them had a chat whereby the boss got the secretary to confirm that indeed she was worried about redundancy as it had happened to her before. He promised her she would never be made redundant, providing her current level of work was maintained.He then went on to say he felt she was capable of making a greater contribution, that she should try to do so and hence fulfil herself and enjoy her work more.

Of course, not everything is so simple. Another boss offered a subordinate a company car if certain agreed targets were achieved. The subordinate worked tremendously well, got the car and then did virtually nothing! This was, of course, not intelligent of the subordinate and a lot was learned of his commitment. But the problem is with the boss. The boss has a duty to create an environment whereby subordinates are motivated to achieve as much as possible, to fulfil themselves as much as possible.

3. *Planning - subordinates*
Determining the most effective way of co-ordinating and actioning those resources needed to complete a task.

Within man-management planning should, as much as possible, be carried out with the people whom it directly affects.

Many mis-communications are created because of the lack of involvement of these people. Most plans are all the better for having an input from them.

Subordinates should be involved as much as possible to determine the resources required to carry out a given task in which they are involved. They should be made aware of the constraints and these should be explained whenever necessary. It is not always necessary to have everyone at all meetings just because they have made a prior contribution, but they should all be made aware of relevant decisions and their input should always be acknowledged.

Timescales and financial constraints should always be explained and agreed. If this is done correctly then the subordinate will have agreed to the resources required to achieve these targets. And if that is done the targets will be met. Have faith.

To play devil's advocate again. What happens if the subordinate does not agree with, for example, a time constraint or what happens if an agreed date is missed?

If the subordinate cannot agree with the time constraint the boss should take the responsibility for the date being met - assuming the boss agrees that it is possible. The subordinate should then either allow the boss to manage the required resources or be allowed to have his own time constraint. The boss should choose which alternative he prefers.

If a due date is not met, what happens? A good subordinate will have kept his boss informed, allowing precautions to be taken. In the worst case when this does not happen the subordinate should be asked as to why the failure occurred. Normally good reasons as opposed to excuses will be given; lessons will have been learned and action taken by the subordinate so that it does not happen again. If it does happen again the boss has a problem. He or she has to determine the reasons, consider all options and decide what to do. Below is just a few of the possible actions to be considered, having first minimised and evaluated the damage.

1. Ask the subordinate again why it has happened again.

2. Give the subordinate a severe telling off. Used sparingly this method can be effective; however, it is rarely motivational and hence should only be used as a last resort.

3. Consider appropriate training. The subordinate and colleagues should be involved in determining what training is required.

4. Give the subordinate the benefit of the doubt (again). Hopefully the boss has already been reasonable in this regard, but it should be considered again.

5. Issue an official warning and state that this is the first step leading towards possible dismissal. This should only be carried out in the most serious of circumstances.

6. Consider demotion. This very often leads to the subordinate leaving the company. It is demotivational, not just for the subordinate.

7. Consider whether or not the subordinate would be better off in a similar role but in a different department. Again this can be demotivational.

8. Counsel colleagues to determine their views as to what to do.

9. Suggest that the subordinate has too much to do and that he or she should encourage a colleague or subordinate to take over some of their work. Assist with the transition.

10. Look at the agreed timescale and re-evaluate whether or not, with the benefit of hindsight, it was reasonable.

There are also other methods of helping the subordinate in terms of planning.

1.   Always get them to set their own objectives.

2.   Always get them to agree a time scale for these objectives, ideally no longer than a week.

3.   Always ensure that the subordinate has the resources required.

4.   Always get the subordinate to set their own priorities. If this is a problem, the boss should give them the information they require so they can do so.

5.   Ensure that the subordinate writes all these things down in a simple format.

If a subordinate gets into these habits he will work happily with the company for years, to everyone's benefit.

4. *Sell - to subordinates*
To motivate someone to buy an idea, product or services that they want.

Selling is fundamental to 5DM and to everything that is done by the 5DM manager. Telling is out almost totally. Persuasion, explaining and asking questions is the only way forward. It does take a little longer at the outset, but very quickly less time is required as the subordinate gains confidence and develops and hence performs better.

Part of the selling process is to point out why the individual should want to carry out their duties to the best of their abilities. They have to want to fulfil themselves and by that is meant to do better, to be innovative.

Recognition of performance is also a part of selling. Being honest and thus trustworthy is a part of selling. In the same way, setting an example is a part of selling. As a boss you have to gain the respect of your subordinates; the way to that is not achieved by knowing all the answers.

Not that anyone does.

The managing director of a certain individual, many years before 5DM had evolved, wanted him to go on a particular training seminar. He knew that the individual would not want to go but felt it was important that he attended.

The MD said to the person that he felt it was necessary that someone should go on the course. He explained why and suggested that a third person should be chosen. The individual agreed that someone should go on the course and, relieved that it was not him, went on to explain how important the subject matter was and why the third person should be chosen.

The MD then stated he was so impressed by the case put forward and the importance that the 'victim' attached to the subject that he should go on the course instead.

Nowadays our 5DM MD would behave slightly differently, but the selling achieved the desired result.

Another very important aspect of this skill is persuading people that they can contribute, they can innovate, that they can make mistakes. If someone has been brought up or has worked in an environment where criticism is the norm, it is going to be some while before they trust a radically different environment.

If all this sounds idealistic, it is. If all this sounds impossible, it is. The only thing wrong with ideals is that they are unachievable. But this does not mean that we should not have ideals. It means that we all have to come to terms with the fact that we are not perfect - try as we may. As we are not perfect we should not expect others to be so. What we should expect from everyone, including ourselves, is that we all do our best. As stated by many others, "Good enough is just not good enough". We must all change, to change we have to learn; to learn we have to be receptive.

So what do we do if someone will not do their best or if their best is just not good enough? Assuming we have been through all the selling, persuading training etc, what happens then?

If after all that; if, after asking the person what the problem is, their performance is still inadequate, the boss has to accept responsibility and take action.

The options are almost infinite because of the infinite variables and situations. But, several things are fundamental to any 5DM solution. First of all this inadequate performance cannot be allowed to continue, second, it is not "somebody's fault", these things happen and the responsibility lies with the boss. Recruitment methods should be examined, the effectiveness of training should be examined, lessons should be learnt. Was too much expected of the individual?

The person concerned should be involved in these discussions. The underlying attitude should be: as no one likes to fail the person concerned cannot be happy.

For this reason, we need to find the person a position where he or she can be happy, hopefully but not necessarily within the same organisation. There is a fulfilling role for everyone, it is everyone's wish that we should all find such a role. If all this is done, the action needed will not be a surprise and it never should be.

5. *Measuring - subordinates*
To determine how effective you are as a 5DM manager.

The measuring of how good one is at managing subordinates can again be undertaken in the normal 5DM way. The boss can prepare a questionnaire around the management skills and ask several people to rank his performance. This should almost certainly be carried out on an anonymous basis.

In all dimensions but especially in this one, secretaries should be involved. Good ones are often diplomatic but they can accurately reflect not only their own, valid views but those of the department or office.

Unlike other dimensions, however, bosses can also be measured in other ways determined by research and experiments carried out over the years. Staff turnover is one very good way. Good bosses have very little staff turnover, bad bosses consistently have a high staff turnover.

The salaries of well run departments or companies tend to be higher than the norm. Other departments within the same company try to poach their staff. Morale is noticeably higher.

Common with the other dimensions any boss of worth will want to regularly measure his effectiveness. He will regularly want to have the opinions of his subordinates and people in all the other dimensions.

SUMMARY OF CHAPTER SEVEN

Managing Subordinates

1. The boss has a responsibility to develop his or her subordinates so that they can fulfil their potential.

2. Bosses should never solve their subordinates' problems.

3. Bosses have lots to learn from subordinates.

4. Bosses should recognise that subordinates want to do a good job and want to be appreciated. If they don't or if they fail, it is the boss' responsibility and it is for the boss to use his authority - but not autocratically.

CHAPTER 8

The 5th Dimension - Managing You

F or most people this will be the most surprising dimension and therefore potentially the most difficult dimension to manage.

Everybody would agree that you are a resource, a human resource and therefore you need managing.

This seems logical and it is; but to many it is unusual, certainly so when considering managing oneself in such a conscious way as is now being proposed. But such conscious management is fundamental to Five Dimensional Management.

Nowhere have we stated that you are the only person to manage you. That would contradict everything within the whole concept. Yet whilst we should welcome being managed by others we must manage ourselves and ultimately must accept the responsibility for what we achieve.

Of course we have bad luck, we all do. Of course we all have lousy bosses, work for lousy companies and have to go through recessions etc. But all of these are management challenges. Identifying problems is only a small part of management; blaming other people or circumstances has nothing to do with management. Coming up with solutions, being innovative and taking intelligent decisions is what Five Dimensional Management is all about.

As with all the other dimensions we are going to end this chapter by measuring our management abilities. In this case, measuring includes achieving pre-determined objectives.

Objectives are essential in management, in all the dimensions and none more so than the fifth. But objectives are not finite and by this we mean that they can and should change.

Obviously, if an objective is achieved we should set ourselves others. Objectives should not be achieved easily but they should be achievable. They should also be part of an overall strategy. Put another way they can be stepping stones on the way to an overall objective or goal. Sometimes they will not be achieved or, worse, will not be achievable.

Assuming that a footballer wants to fulfil himself, he might set as his overall objective his desire to play for his country. His first stepping stone may be to become a professional footballer, the next to get into the first team and then to play for his country. Each one is an objective going towards his overall aim. Whenever he peaks (as we all do), he has reached his final objective, he has fulfilled himself.

However, if after playing football for three years, he lost a leg he would have to set himself new objectives. He would not have failed. This is an obvious example but one that we can use in all aspects of everyday work. When you are 21 you may well want to be Managing Director of the Virgin Corporation, at 41 you may have realised that you will never achieve this. If it is now unachievable, you have not failed; you have merely learnt and hence you have to set yourself new goals.

If at the age of 61 you still want to be Managing Director of Virgin but you still remain the maintenance supervisor, you need to come to terms with the fact that you have peaked in terms of your career (not life).

It has been said many times that the journey is often better than arriving and we tend to agree. The setting of goals is very exciting. The striving, the learning, the achievement of the stepping stones is very rewarding. The sense of purpose and direction is very motivational so remember to enjoy the successes. But then set yourself the next objective.

You can't succeed without an objective. If you really do your best and don't achieve the goal, the goal was wrong.

This brings us to another very important item in terms of managing yourself. Be honest with yourself, do not delude yourself. If in doubt assume that you are, if anything, optimistic. Be realistic about your achievements. If you are a maintenance supervisor at the age of 61, enjoy it, believe that you are worthy. Know that you are fulfilled, be happy and content.

Better to be fulfilled carrying out a role to the best of your ability than be promoted to the next level and fail. At the same time, if you are going to do a job do it honestly, to the very best of your ability. Otherwise you will always wonder what you could have achieved if you had.

How are we to manage ourselves and ensure that we are fulfilled?

Before managing ourselves through the five management skills, we need to come to terms with ourselves, to know ourselves in terms of the four personality types. We need to acknowledge our strengths and weaknesses. Despite how we view ourselves and can justify our actions, we should read the characteristics of our personality type and accept that that is how we are. Most of us are very worthwhile people whose strengths far exceed our weaknesses; nevertheless, we need to manage these weak areas whilst maximising our strengths.

1. *Communication - with yourself*
   Getting the right message to the right person at the right time in the right way to get the right results.

   Talking to yourself can be useful but be careful, anyone listening may think you are completely mad.

Funnily enough, many people do 'talk' to themselves, particularly when preparing for a speech or presentation. It's a good idea. But within Five Dimensional Management there are probably better methods of managing yourself.

A good way is to write things down. It's simple and obvious but it is also very effective. If you write down what you are going to do and by when, not only will you have a better chance of remembering it but you will feel more committed to achieving the aim.

The best managers are the best organisers. The best organisers write things down and in a logical, organised way. There are all sorts of systems available to help and most of them do so.

One of the ways of using the written word is to put things in such a place that you regularly come across them and get reminded of a valuable message. Examples of this include the director of a public limited company who read the same management book on every summer holiday. Another is the New Zealand cricketer, Richard Hadlee who had some initials on his kit bag to remind of what to him was an inspirational message.

Communicating with yourself also means receiving information that you have chosen. Reading books is one such communication. Another is the ever increasing use of audio cassettes so that you can receive pre-selected messages whilst driving. When using these methods be intelligent and don't just think short term. If you are a very successful salesman don't just read sales books. Assuming you want to be promoted into sales management etc, start receiving management messages. On the assumption that you sell to managers you might even learn something to improve as a salesman by knowing them and what they do better.

If you want to be promoted, communicate the message. Be enthusiastic, wear the right sort of clothes, length of hair, take the initiative. Demonstrate your capabilities. Don't wait to be asked.

2. *Motivation - of yourself*
**The process by which someone does something because
they want to.**

Motivation again dovetails in with the other skills. To be
motivated and to motivate yourself you have to have objectives.
Only then can you determine the steps to be taken along the
way and then the tools required to achieve those steps.

Virtually all things are achievable if you have the motivation,
the real desire to achieve them. If you really do have the desire
and if you are prepared to work very hard you will almost
certainly achieve.

With a degree of natural ability in addition you will excel in
your chosen field.

Too many people are not prepared to make the effort.
Despite what they say about themselves, they do not really want
to achieve the goal badly enough.

If you really do not want to achieve, to be ambitious, then
fine. But realise that time is passing you by and that the
responsibility for that decision lies with you. You cannot blame
someone else for the decision.

Once you have set yourself goals don't worry about the 'how';
don't let the 'how' deter you from setting the goal you really
want. Set your goal and take the first step, don't worry about
anything else.

Self-motivation is another topic on which many books have
been written. It all revolves around strength of character, inner
confidence, an inner belief, an ability not to give up. In many
ways that is what intelligence is, because that is what intelligent
people have or do. Don't mistake strength of character for
talking, don't mistake arrogance for inner strength; neither
could be further from the truth.

Motivation can be developed and enhanced. It can be

developed from achievement, from genuine praise and the sincere admiration of others. Respecting people for who they are and what they have achieved can be inspirational and motivational. Jealousy is equally as powerful but in a negative way.

To begin fulfilling yourself, set yourself objectives that you want to achieve and that you know you can achieve, with effort. Don't worry about the detail, just believe it, just do it!

3. *Planning - yourself*
Determining the most effective way of co-ordinating and actioning those resources needed to complete a task.

In previous dimensions, planning has revolved around discipline and time management. Exactly the same message needs to be imparted in this dimension. Be organised, use diaries, reminders etc. If you say you're going to do it, do it. Always put a timescale on any such commitment.

Another less obvious aspect of planning is to make use of all the available resources. Do not believe that you have to do everything. Worse, do not believe that there is no one who can do the task as well as you.

As with management as a whole, judgement is required but not every single task needs doing to perfection. For example, if your time costs £20 per hour there is little point spending two hours looking for the missing £10. Judgement, intelligence and common sense should always prevail.

So in a more practical way if you are asked to make 10 units in 10 hours, don't try to make 12. Organise your time and your other resources to do what is asked and then do something else worthwhile or just make yourself available. Equally if you can make the 10 units within seven hours do not just use the available time up, ie, don't waste the three hours. Time is valuable, use it constructively. If you do decide to waste time, people will notice and even if they can't prove it, they will manage you accordingly. Be honest with yourself because you know the truth. Which of us can say we could not work harder? Very few.

There are any number of techniques to assist in planning of any type. Different people in different situations make use of all of them at different times. Basically the secret is to break the goal down into simple realistic steps.

A man who had built his own house whilst raising a family and running a business was asked how on earth he had achieved it. He replied that he was not sure, he had only thought and planned for the next week's work.

Do not be put off by looking too much at the final step to be taken, just concentrate on the next one. Take one step at a time, just plan for that next step.

4. *Sell - to yourself*
To motivate someone to buy an idea, product or service they want.

Selling to oneself is a strange idea but if called persuasion it begins to make more sense.

Most people need persuasion that they can achieve their own goals, their own dreams. We have to believe it is possible, even though it may not be probable as things look at the outset.

Don't just rely on others to do this. Look hard at yourself. Examine what you have achieved, compare yourself to others and be honest about what you have achieved to-date. Know that with some effort the required result is achieveable. If you're not sure then you have to make a greater effort or reduce your goals. If you know what is required, you are persuaded, you will have persuaded yourself.

Other people's opinions are of course important, but whether good or bad only rely on those people you know and respect. Be persuaded by them alone. The opinions of people who do not know you, that you do not know or of people you have no valid reason to respect, are worthless.

As part of this self-persuasion enjoy and celebrate your successes. Acknowledge that you have achieved and enjoy the first sight of the next step. This celebration need not be an external thing or one that involves others. Equally the achievement does not need to be held in high regard by anyone else other than you.

Two examples spring to mind. The first is a person who, whenever he succeeds, feels slightly deflated as he thinks that because he achieved the goal it must have been easy, one that anyone could achieve.

The second person bought himself a music cassette every time he obtained an order and wrote the customer's name inside the cover. Every time he heard his favourite music he, and only he, was reminded of his successes. We all do better if we feel good especially about ourselves.

5. *Measuring - yourself*
To determine how effective you are as a 5DM manager.

Identify one or two people who you really respect and admire. Tell them that you hold them in high regard and that you would value their opinion as to your management skills. Some people will still find it difficult to do so. Do not ask them to praise or criticise. Ask them to rank your skills and listen very carefully when they talk. Especially when they talk about you and your work. Do not believe you cannot improve on your best skills. Do not believe you are incapable of improving at your worst. Keep it all in proportion. Continually try to improve but with one step at a time. Even a small improvement is worthwhile.

The traditional Five Dimensional Management methods should also be used with the use of a questionnaire. Again the questions should revolve around the basic management skills. Having got the results - take action.

'Name' wants your opinion of her management abilities; could you take two minutes to rank the following management skills? Put a 1 by her best management quality, 2 by her second best and so on down to number 9.

Ranking

1. She is a good, clear speaker. ☐
2. She is a concise, accurate writer of letters, memos etc. ☐
3. She is always helpful and willing. ☐
4. She is always well dressed and behaves in a
   businesslike way. ☐
5. She is well organised and tidy. ☐
6. She is persuasive. ☐
7. She is motivated. ☐
8. She learns quickly. ☐
9. She gets on well with her colleagues. ☐

SUMMARY OF CHAPTER EIGHT

Managing You

1. Set yourself realistic objectives on the way to achieving your fabulous goals.

2. Be honest about yourself. If in doubt ask a friend and assume that, if anything, you are more optimistic than them.

3. Break your goals down into simple achievable steps. Only worry about the next one.

4. Accept total responsibility for what you achieve and celebrate each stepping stone.

CHAPTER 9

Synergy And The 5DM Philosophy Away From Work

F ive Dimensional Management is an ideal. Some will undoubtedly feel it necessary to criticise it for being so. An ideal such as Five Dimensional Management is not achievable because none of us is perfect or anywhere near it. What Five Dimensional Management enables us to do is to manage our imperfections, to come to terms with them and yet to never accept that things and certainly man-management skills cannot be improved. Not only are we imperfect but also the people we are managing, including ourselves, are continually changing. That is the challenge, that is the thrill.

If you do not accept that, then you are not a manager, let alone a Five Dimensional Manager.

As with all ideals, a 'believer' may speculate as to what it would be like if everyone believed as he or she does.

Without becoming complacent or arrogant let us imagine what it would be like if everyone was a Five Dimensional Manager.

Everybody would see themselves in a far more equal way. Elitism would be minimised, status would not be an ego problem. Everyone would manage everyone else in a conscious way but not at the expense of their instincts or reactions. These would always remain and be used. But they would only be one or two of the options being considered.

We would all give due consideration to our man-management problems rather than just relying on previous experience. We would all exercise our brain trying to come up with 20 options. We would all help each other with these options. We would all help each other generally.

In Five Dimensional Management everyone wants to do better. We are all doing our best, our best is good enough and yet we all want to do a little bit better. We all want to learn and grow.

As a subordinate or colleague we are not going to wait to be told what to do. We are going to come up with as many ideas as our boss because we are just as intelligent even if we don't have as much overall experience. On the other hand, we have experiences and knowledge that our boss does not have.

As a boss we believe that your main aim is to create an environment whereby your subordinates can achieve and fulfil themselves. Only if they fulfil themselves can you do likewise.

The way to help subordinates fulfil themselves is for them to resolve as many of their problems as possible. They should not look to others as the source of all knowledge. They should not look to others to solve their problems. They should look to you for support, genuine praise, respect and honesty.

As Five Dimensional Managers we acknowledge that we are all interdependent upon each other. Everyone we come into contact with can be helped by us and can in turn help us.

The converse is also true, we can all make each other's life a misery, we can all tell someone that they are useless. Being destructive is commonplace in the 90s, an attitude created, or at the very least influenced, by the media getting things out of proportion. There are too many people laughing at others, rather than with them. It's become commonplace to be critical.

If we could get everyone to be positive, honest, confident and trusting; if we could get everyone to give 5% of their time to helping someone else for no other reason than it makes both people feel good, the results would be incredible.

It's called synergy. Impossible? No. In fact synergy has been experienced by many people. Often in fairly small groups and only for a limited period. It often happens in small groups because the chances of it happening are linked to the number of people involved. The greater the number of people, the less chance of synergy occurring.

It only happens for a limited time for several reasons. Often it ends when the team has achieved the goal, climbed the mountain or whatever. Often it ends because of the success of the team, whereby someone feels it necessary to break the team up. Another reason is that factors, possibly not realised, have changed.

Examples of synergy are plentiful and legendary. For example, the human spirit which survived the prisoner of war camps. Or, the spirit which enabled James Hunt and the Hesketh team to beat all the £multi-million organisations to win the Formula One World Championship in 1976.

If you have never seen or experienced synergy you will not believe it. If you have, you will never forget it and it will inspire you for the rest of your life. You will always be seeking it again. And you will perform better because you are seeking it.

This same attitude can be just as useful away from work and to those who don't go to work. Whether you are at work or not, managing different people in different ways is a good idea. To do so intelligently and consciously will make life better and more enjoyable. Continually exercising your brain and being creative can become a lovely habit to get into.

If all parents started thinking of children, as they progress from being a young baby, in a Five Dimensional Management way, the benefits would be considerable: "Always praise behaviour you want repeated".

Involve them as much as possible in solving their own problems without leaving them to it. And without always telling them what to do.

Teach them that constraints are not restraints. Teach them that resources are finite but that being creative is not a problem either.

Teach them to set goals, to shoot for the moon. Teach them to manage disappointment and to celebrate success, however small. Show them that to help others is to be strong.

Housewives are managers because they do all the things that managers do, all the things in this book - or they should do. As long as they take responsibility for their own actions and for what they achieve, they are managers. Just like anyone else.

If everyone behaved in these ways, if everyone put as much effort into being positive and creative as many do into being negative and critical the world would be a better place. If we all stopped feasting on the 'gutter' press, stopped watching television and did something creative instead, the world would be a better place. No one person can change the world but everyone can improve their world. However small the step that you take is, it's a step in the right direction.

FOR FUTHER INFORMATION regarding
Five Dimensional Management and the associated
products listed below, please contact:

Five Dimensional Management
15-17 The Broadway
Old Hatfield
Herts. AL9 5HZ
ENGLAND

5DM Job Evaluations
5DM Appraisal Systems
5DM Recruitment and Interviewing Seminar
5DM Sales Seminars
5DM Audio Cassettes
5DM Introductory Seminars
5DM Outplacement Counselling
5DM Management Consultancy
5DM Presentation Seminars